British Politics: A Very Short Introduction

VERY SHORT INTRODUCTIONS are for anyone wanting a stimulating and accessible way in to a new subject. They are written by experts and have been translated into more than 40 different languages. The series began in 1995 and now covers a wide variety of topics in every discipline. The VSI library contains nearly 400 volumes—a Very Short Introduction to everything from Indian philosophy to psychology and American history—and continues to grow in every subject area.

Very Short Introductions available now:

ACCOUNTING Christopher Nobes
ADVERTISING Winston Fletcher
AFRICAN HISTORY John Parker and
  Richard Rathbone
AGNOSTICISM Robin Le Poidevin
ALEXANDER THE GREAT
  Hugh Bowden
AMERICAN HISTORY Paul S. Boyer
AMERICAN IMMIGRATION
  David A. Gerber
AMERICAN POLITICAL PARTIES
  AND ELECTIONS L. Sandy Maisel
AMERICAN POLITICS Richard M. Valelly
THE AMERICAN PRESIDENCY
  Charles O. Jones
ANAESTHESIA Aidan O'Donnell
ANARCHISM Colin Ward
ANCIENT EGYPT Ian Shaw
ANCIENT GREECE Paul Cartledge
THE ANCIENT NEAR EAST
  Amanda H. Podany
ANCIENT PHILOSOPHY Julia Annas
ANCIENT WARFARE Harry Sidebottom
ANGELS David Albert Jones
ANGLICANISM Mark Chapman
THE ANGLO-SAXON AGE John Blair
THE ANIMAL KINGDOM Peter Holland
ANIMAL RIGHTS David DeGrazia
THE ANTARCTIC Klaus Dodds
ANTISEMITISM Steven Beller
ANXIETY Daniel Freeman and
  Jason Freeman
THE APOCRYPHAL GOSPELS
  Paul Foster
ARCHAEOLOGY Paul Bahn

ARCHITECTURE Andrew Ballantyne
ARISTOCRACY William Doyle
ARISTOTLE Jonathan Barnes
ART HISTORY Dana Arnold
ART THEORY Cynthia Freeland
ASTROBIOLOGY David C. Catling
ATHEISM Julian Baggini
AUGUSTINE Henry Chadwick
AUSTRALIA Kenneth Morgan
AUTISM Uta Frith
THE AVANT GARDE David Cottington
THE AZTECS Davíd Carrasco
BACTERIA Sebastian G. B. Amyes
BARTHES Jonathan Culler
THE BEATS David Sterritt
BEAUTY Roger Scruton
BESTSELLERS John Sutherland
THE BIBLE John Riches
BIBLICAL ARCHAEOLOGY Eric H. Cline
BIOGRAPHY Hermione Lee
THE BLUES Elijah Wald
THE BOOK OF MORMON Terryl Givens
BORDERS Alexander C. Diener and
  Joshua Hagen
THE BRAIN Michael O'Shea
THE BRITISH CONSTITUTION
  Martin Loughlin
THE BRITISH EMPIRE Ashley Jackson
BRITISH POLITICS Anthony Wright
BUDDHA Michael Carrithers
BUDDHISM Damien Keown
BUDDHIST ETHICS Damien Keown
CANCER Nicholas James
CAPITALISM James Fulcher
CATHOLICISM Gerald O'Collins

CAUSATION Stephen Mumford and
    Rani Lill Anjum
THE CELL Terence Allen and
    Graham Cowling
THE CELTS Barry Cunliffe
CHAOS Leonard Smith
CHILDREN'S LITERATURE
    Kimberley Reynolds
CHINESE LITERATURE Sabina Knight
CHOICE THEORY Michael Allingham
CHRISTIAN ART Beth Williamson
CHRISTIAN ETHICS D. Stephen Long
CHRISTIANITY Linda Woodhead
CITIZENSHIP Richard Bellamy
CIVIL ENGINEERING David Muir Wood
CLASSICAL LITERATURE William Allan
CLASSICAL MYTHOLOGY Helen Morales
CLASSICS Mary Beard and John Henderson
CLAUSEWITZ Michael Howard
CLIMATE Mark Maslin
THE COLD WAR Robert McMahon
COLONIAL AMERICA Alan Taylor
COLONIAL LATIN AMERICAN
    LITERATURE Rolena Adorno
COMEDY Matthew Bevis
COMMUNISM Leslie Holmes
COMPLEXITY John H. Holland
THE COMPUTER Darrel Ince
THE CONQUISTADORS Matthew
    Restall and Felipe Fernández-Armesto
CONSCIENCE Paul Strohm
CONSCIOUSNESS Susan Blackmore
CONTEMPORARY ART Julian Stallabrass
CONTEMPORARY FICTION
    Robert Eaglestone
CONTINENTAL PHILOSOPHY
    Simon Critchley
CORAL REEFS Charles Sheppard
COSMOLOGY Peter Coles
CRITICAL THEORY Stephen Eric Bronner
THE CRUSADES Christopher Tyerman
CRYPTOGRAPHY Fred Piper and
    Sean Murphy
THE CULTURAL
    REVOLUTION Richard Curt Kraus
DADA AND SURREALISM
    David Hopkins
DARWIN Jonathan Howard
THE DEAD SEA SCROLLS Timothy Lim
DEMOCRACY Bernard Crick
DERRIDA Simon Glendinning

DESCARTES Tom Sorell
DESERTS Nick Middleton
DESIGN John Heskett
DEVELOPMENTAL BIOLOGY
    Lewis Wolpert
THE DEVIL Darren Oldridge
DIASPORA Kevin Kenny
DICTIONARIES Lynda Mugglestone
DINOSAURS David Norman
DIPLOMACY Joseph M. Siracusa
DOCUMENTARY FILM
    Patricia Aufderheide
DREAMING J. Allan Hobson
DRUGS Leslie Iversen
DRUIDS Barry Cunliffe
EARLY MUSIC Thomas Forrest Kelly
THE EARTH Martin Redfern
ECONOMICS Partha Dasgupta
EDUCATION Gary Thomas
EGYPTIAN MYTH Geraldine Pinch
EIGHTEENTH-CENTURY
    BRITAIN Paul Langford
THE ELEMENTS Philip Ball
EMOTION Dylan Evans
EMPIRE Stephen Howe
ENGELS Terrell Carver
ENGINEERING David Blockley
ENGLISH LITERATURE Jonathan Bate
ENVIRONMENTAL ECONOMICS
    Stephen Smith
EPIDEMIOLOGY Rodolfo Saracci
ETHICS Simon Blackburn
THE EUROPEAN UNION John Pinder
    and Simon Usherwood
EVOLUTION Brian and
    Deborah Charlesworth
EXISTENTIALISM Thomas Flynn
THE EYE Michael Land
FAMILY LAW Jonathan Herring
FASCISM Kevin Passmore
FASHION Rebecca Arnold
FEMINISM Margaret Walters
FILM Michael Wood
FILM MUSIC Kathryn Kalinak
THE FIRST WORLD WAR
    Michael Howard
FOLK MUSIC Mark Slobin
FOOD John Krebs
FORENSIC PSYCHOLOGY David Canter
FORENSIC SCIENCE Jim Fraser
FOSSILS Keith Thomson

FOUCAULT Gary Gutting
FRACTALS Kenneth Falconer
FREE SPEECH Nigel Warburton
FREE WILL Thomas Pink
FRENCH LITERATURE John D. Lyons
THE FRENCH REVOLUTION
    William Doyle
FREUD Anthony Storr
FUNDAMENTALISM Malise Ruthven
GALAXIES John Gribbin
GALILEO Stillman Drake
GAME THEORY Ken Binmore
GANDHI Bhikhu Parekh
GENIUS Andrew Robinson
GEOGRAPHY John Matthews and
    David Herbert
GEOPOLITICS Klaus Dodds
GERMAN LITERATURE Nicholas Boyle
GERMAN PHILOSOPHY
    Andrew Bowie
GLOBAL CATASTROPHES Bill McGuire
GLOBAL ECONOMIC HISTORY
    Robert C. Allen
GLOBAL WARMING Mark Maslin
GLOBALIZATION Manfred Steger
THE GOTHIC Nick Groom
GOVERNANCE Mark Bevir
THE GREAT DEPRESSION AND THE
    NEW DEAL Eric Rauchway
HABERMAS James Gordon Finlayson
HAPPINESS Daniel M. Haybron
HEGEL Peter Singer
HEIDEGGER Michael Inwood
HERODOTUS Jennifer T. Roberts
HIEROGLYPHS Penelope Wilson
HINDUISM Kim Knott
HISTORY John H. Arnold
THE HISTORY OF ASTRONOMY
    Michael Hoskin
THE HISTORY OF LIFE
    Michael Benton
THE HISTORY OF
    MATHEMATICS Jacqueline Stedall
THE HISTORY OF MEDICINE
    William Bynum
THE HISTORY OF TIME
    Leofranc Holford-Strevens
HIV/AIDS Alan Whiteside
HOBBES Richard Tuck
HORMONES Martin Luck
HUMAN EVOLUTION Bernard Wood

HUMAN RIGHTS Andrew Clapham
HUMANISM Stephen Law
HUME A. J. Ayer
HUMOUR Noël Carroll
THE ICE AGE Jamie Woodward
IDEOLOGY Michael Freeden
INDIAN PHILOSOPHY Sue Hamilton
INFORMATION Luciano Floridi
INNOVATION Mark Dodgson and
    David Gann
INTELLIGENCE Ian J. Deary
INTERNATIONAL
    MIGRATION Khalid Koser
INTERNATIONAL RELATIONS
    Paul Wilkinson
INTERNATIONAL
    SECURITY Christopher S. Browning
ISLAM Malise Ruthven
ISLAMIC HISTORY Adam Silverstein
ITALIAN LITERATURE Peter
    Hainsworth and David Robey
JESUS Richard Bauckham
JOURNALISM Ian Hargreaves
JUDAISM Norman Solomon
JUNG Anthony Stevens
KABBALAH Joseph Dan
KAFKA Ritchie Robertson
KANT Roger Scruton
KEYNES Robert Skidelsky
KIERKEGAARD Patrick Gardiner
THE KORAN Michael Cook
LANDSCAPE ARCHITECTURE
    Ian H. Thompson
LANDSCAPES AND
    GEOMORPHOLOGY
    Andrew Goudie and Heather Viles
LANGUAGES Stephen R. Anderson
LATE ANTIQUITY Gillian Clark
LAW Raymond Wacks
THE LAWS OF THERMODYNAMICS
    Peter Atkins
LEADERSHIP Keith Grint
LINCOLN Allen C. Guelzo
LINGUISTICS Peter Matthews
LITERARY THEORY Jonathan Culler
LOCKE John Dunn
LOGIC Graham Priest
MACHIAVELLI Quentin Skinner
MADNESS Andrew Scull
MAGIC Owen Davies
MAGNA CARTA Nicholas Vincent

MAGNETISM Stephen Blundell
MALTHUS Donald Winch
MANAGEMENT John Hendry
MAO Delia Davin
MARINE BIOLOGY Philip V. Mladenov
THE MARQUIS DE SADE John Phillips
MARTIN LUTHER Scott H. Hendrix
MARTYRDOM Jolyon Mitchell
MARX Peter Singer
MATHEMATICS Timothy Gowers
THE MEANING OF LIFE Terry Eagleton
MEDICAL ETHICS Tony Hope
MEDICAL LAW Charles Foster
MEDIEVAL BRITAIN John
   Gillingham and Ralph A. Griffiths
MEMORY Jonathan K. Foster
METAPHYSICS Stephen Mumford
MICHAEL FARADAY Frank A.J.L. James
MICROECONOMICS Avinash Dixit
MODERN ART David Cottington
MODERN CHINA Rana Mitter
MODERN FRANCE Vanessa R. Schwartz
MODERN IRELAND Senia Pašeta
MODERN JAPAN Christopher Goto-Jones
MODERN LATIN AMERICAN
   LITERATURE
   Roberto González Echevarría
MODERN WAR Richard English
MODERNISM Christopher Butler
MOLECULES Philip Ball
THE MONGOLS Morris Rossabi
MORMONISM Richard Lyman Bushman
MUHAMMAD Jonathan A.C. Brown
MULTICULTURALISM Ali Rattansi
MUSIC Nicholas Cook
MYTH Robert A. Segal
THE NAPOLEONIC WARS
   Mike Rapport
NATIONALISM Steven Grosby
NELSON MANDELA Elleke Boehmer
NEOLIBERALISM Manfred Steger and
   Ravi Roy
NETWORKS Guido Caldarelli
   and Michele Catanzaro
THE NEW TESTAMENT
   Luke Timothy Johnson
THE NEW TESTAMENT AS
   LITERATURE Kyle Keefer
NEWTON Robert Iliffe
NIETZSCHE Michael Tanner

NINETEENTH-CENTURY
   BRITAIN Christopher Harvie and
   H. C. G. Matthew
THE NORMAN CONQUEST
   George Garnett
NORTH AMERICAN
   INDIANS Theda Perdue
   and Michael D. Green
NORTHERN IRELAND
   Marc Mulholland
NOTHING Frank Close
NUCLEAR POWER Maxwell Irvine
NUCLEAR WEAPONS
   Joseph M. Siracusa
NUMBERS Peter M. Higgins
NUTRITION David A. Bender
OBJECTIVITY Stephen Gaukroger
THE OLD TESTAMENT
   Michael D. Coogan
THE ORCHESTRA D. Kern Holoman
ORGANIZATIONS Mary Jo Hatch
PAGANISM Owen Davies
THE PALESTINIAN-ISRAELI CONFLICT
   Martin Bunton
PARTICLE PHYSICS Frank Close
PAUL E. P. Sanders
PENTECOSTALISM William K. Kay
THE PERIODIC TABLE Eric R. Scerri
PHILOSOPHY Edward Craig
PHILOSOPHY OF LAW Raymond Wacks
PHILOSOPHY OF SCIENCE
   Samir Okasha
PHOTOGRAPHY Steve Edwards
PLAGUE Paul Slack
PLANETS David A. Rothery
PLANTS Timothy Walker
PLATO Julia Annas
POLITICAL PHILOSOPHY David Miller
POLITICS Kenneth Minogue
POSTCOLONIALISM Robert Young
POSTMODERNISM Christopher Butler
POSTSTRUCTURALISM
   Catherine Belsey
PREHISTORY Chris Gosden
PRESOCRATIC PHILOSOPHY
   Catherine Osborne
PRIVACY Raymond Wacks
PROBABILITY John Haigh
PROGRESSIVISM Walter Nugent
PROTESTANTISM Mark A. Noll

PSYCHIATRY Tom Burns
PSYCHOLOGY Gillian Butler
    and Freda McManus
PURITANISM Francis J. Bremer
THE QUAKERS Pink Dandelion
QUANTUM THEORY John Polkinghorne
RACISM Ali Rattansi
RADIOACTIVITY Claudio Tuniz
RASTAFARI Ennis B. Edmonds
THE REAGAN REVOLUTION Gil Troy
REALITY Jan Westerhoff
THE REFORMATION Peter Marshall
RELATIVITY Russell Stannard
RELIGION IN AMERICA Timothy Beal
THE RENAISSANCE Jerry Brotton
RENAISSANCE ART
    Geraldine A. Johnson
REVOLUTIONS Jack A. Goldstone
RHETORIC Richard Toye
RISK Baruch Fischhoff and John Kadvany
RIVERS Nick Middleton
ROBOTICS Alan Winfield
ROMAN BRITAIN Peter Salway
THE ROMAN EMPIRE Christopher Kelly
THE ROMAN REPUBLIC
    David M. Gwynn
ROMANTICISM Michael Ferber
ROUSSEAU Robert Wokler
RUSSELL A. C. Grayling
RUSSIAN HISTORY Geoffrey Hosking
RUSSIAN LITERATURE Catriona Kelly
THE RUSSIAN REVOLUTION
    S. A. Smith
SCHIZOPHRENIA Chris Frith and
    Eve Johnstone
SCHOPENHAUER
    Christopher Janaway
SCIENCE AND RELIGION
    Thomas Dixon
SCIENCE FICTION David Seed
THE SCIENTIFIC REVOLUTION
    Lawrence M. Principe
SCOTLAND Rab Houston
SEXUALITY Véronique Mottier
SHAKESPEARE Germaine Greer
SIKHISM Eleanor Nesbitt
THE SILK ROAD James A. Millward
SLEEP Steven W. Lockley and
    Russell G. Foster

SOCIAL AND CULTURAL
    ANTHROPOLOGY
    John Monaghan and Peter Just
SOCIALISM Michael Newman
SOCIOLINGUISTICS John Edwards
SOCIOLOGY Steve Bruce
SOCRATES C. C. W. Taylor
THE SOVIET UNION Stephen Lovell
THE SPANISH CIVIL WAR
    Helen Graham
SPANISH LITERATURE Jo Labanyi
SPINOZA Roger Scruton
SPIRITUALITY Philip Sheldrake
STARS Andrew King
STATISTICS David J. Hand
STEM CELLS Jonathan Slack
STUART BRITAIN John Morrill
SUPERCONDUCTIVITY Stephen Blundell
SYMMETRY Ian Stewart
TEETH Peter S. Ungar
TERRORISM Charles Townshend
THEOLOGY David F. Ford
THOMAS AQUINAS Fergus Kerr
THOUGHT Tim Bayne
TIBETAN BUDDHISM
    Matthew T. Kapstein
TOCQUEVILLE Harvey C. Mansfield
TRAGEDY Adrian Poole
THE TROJAN WAR Eric H. Cline
TRUST Katherine Hawley
THE TUDORS John Guy
TWENTIETH-CENTURY
    BRITAIN Kenneth O. Morgan
THE UNITED NATIONS
    Jussi M. Hanhimäki
THE U.S. CONGRESS Donald A. Ritchie
THE U.S. SUPREME COURT
    Linda Greenhouse
UTOPIANISM Lyman Tower Sargent
THE VIKINGS Julian Richards
VIRUSES Dorothy H. Crawford
WITCHCRAFT Malcolm Gaskill
WITTGENSTEIN A. C. Grayling
WORK Stephen Fineman
WORLD MUSIC Philip Bohlman
THE WORLD TRADE
    ORGANIZATION Amrita Narlikar
WRITING AND SCRIPT
    Andrew Robinson

Tony Wright

BRITISH POLITICS
A Very Short Introduction

OXFORD
UNIVERSITY PRESS

OXFORD

UNIVERSITY PRESS

Great Clarendon Street, Oxford, OX2 6DP,
United Kingdom

Oxford University Press is a department of the University of Oxford.
It furthers the University's objective of excellence in research, scholarship,
and education by publishing worldwide. Oxford is a registered trade mark of
Oxford University Press in the UK and in certain other countries

First Edition published in 2003
This edition published 2013

Impression: 5

British Library Cataloguing in Publication Data

Data available

ISBN 978-0-19-966110-7

Printed in Great Britain by
Ashford Colour Press Ltd, Gosport, Hampshire

For Moira
(also Very Short)

Contents

Preface xii

List of illustrations xiii

1 The Britishness of British politics 1

2 The constitution: old and new 17

3 Arguing: the political conversation 35

4 Governing: the strong centre? 52

5 Representing: is the party over? 70

6 Accounting: heckling the steamroller? 86

7 The end of British politics? 104

Further reading 121

Index 125

Preface

In preparing a new edition of this little book, I have taken the opportunity not just to bring it up to date, adding and deleting material in every chapter, but also to review and revise some of the judgements I make in the light of new developments and changing political circumstances. The concluding chapter is entirely new and offers an assessment of the contemporary condition—and future prospects—of British politics.

When I wrote the first edition of this book I was a Member of Parliament, having previously been a political academic. In writing this new edition I am no longer a Member of Parliament, but I am again (at least in part) a political academic. I hope the combination of theory and practice—the academic and the practical—is reflected in this account of British politics. That, at least, has been my aim.

Tony Wright

List of illustrations

1 'envied and enviable...':
Winston Churchill eulogizes
Britain's political system
(1945) **3**
Imperial War Museum (neg no.
MII26392)

2 Britain, which Britain?
A poster in the Second World
War supplies one answer **9**
Imperial War Museum (Art.IWM
PST 14887)

3 The 'balanced' constitution of
King, Lords, and Commons
is represented in this
18th-century engraving **22**
Engraving, unknown artist, c.1774.
© The Trustees of the British Museum

4 Reforming the machine
(*Economist*, 18 April 1998) **31**
Economist, 18 April 1998 © David
Simmons

5 Attlee and Thatcher: making
and unmaking the post-war
settlement **44**
top: Hulton Archives/Getty Images
bottom: © Bettmann/Corbis

6 New Labour's 'big tent'
(Chris Riddell,
The Observer, 3 October
1999) **47**
Copyright Guardian News & Media
Ltd 1999. www.guardian.co.uk

7 The last bus (or boat, or
train) to Europe has been
regularly sighted, as this
Low cartoon from the
1950s shows (*Manchester
Guardian*, 10 October
1956) **49**
David Low, *Manchester Guardian*,
10 October 1956 © Evening Standard/
Centre for the Study of Cartoons
and Caricature, University of Kent,
Canterbury

8 The Queen (Victoria)
dissolving Parliament (*Punch*,
1847) **56**
Richard Doyle, *Punch*, August 1847.
Reproduced with permission of Punch
Ltd.

9 Tony Blair buries Cabinet government (Richard Willson, *The Times*, 5 January 1998) **59**
British Cartoon Archive

10 'Find me a baby to kiss': Labour candidates canvassing, Cardiff, 1945 **75**
Daily Herald Archive/NMPFT/ Science and Society Picture Library

11 Winner takes all (*The Guardian*, 26 May 1990) **77**
Copyright Guardian News & Media Ltd 1990. www.guardian.co.uk

12 Whipping them in: this is an example of the 'whip' that goes to MPs from the Chief Whip of their party every week when the Commons is in session **94**

13 'There is always the House of Lords...' (Peter Brookes, *The Times*, 12 July 2012) **101**
Peter Brookes/The Times/NI Syndication

14 'A new politics'? David Cameron and Nick Clegg enter coalition, May 2010 **107**
Matt Cardy/Stringer/Getty Images News

15 'Or new tensions?' (Gary Barker, *The Guardian*, 5 January, 2012) **108**
© Gary Barker

Chapter 1
The Britishness of British politics

> British people would defend to the death the right of a worker to
> withdraw his labour, but they draw the line at strikes.
>
> (Michael Frayn)

Try this game. You have to fill in the blank.

French wine
Italian food
German cars
British—

Not easy, is it? One of my children suggested 'humour', but that
could scarcely be a British gift to the world if nobody else can
understand the joke. Another came up with 'language', which
would be the obvious candidate except for the fact that it is not
English but *British* that we are talking about (a characteristic
confusion that it will be necessary to say something more about
shortly). So (as my children put it) what's the clever-clog answer
then?

There is a good case to be made for 'politics' or 'government'. This
is not an original answer. Indeed it has long been held (not least
by the British) that Britain has displayed a particular approach to
politics that has offered lessons to the world in making

government work. 'This country's distinctive contribution to civilisation', proclaimed the *Daily Telegraph* not so very long ago, 'has been the development of stable institutions of representative government' (19 December 1997). There is plenty to unpick in such a statement (which country precisely? what kind of stability? does representative mean democratic?), but it faithfully echoes a long line of such judgements about the political genius and blessings of the British.

These judgements have been delivered by domestic voices and by foreign observers; by rhetorical politicians and by dispassionate scholars; and by radicals and conservatives. A quick sample might include the following. In 1865 the radical John Bright famously described the country as the 'Mother of Parliaments'. At the end of the Second World War, Prime Minister Winston Churchill told the House of Commons:

> If it be true, as has been said, that every country gets the form of government it deserves, we may certainly flatter ourselves. The wisdom of our ancestors has led us to an envied and enviable situation. We have the strongest Parliament in the world. We have the oldest, the most famous, the most secure, the most serviceable monarchy in the world. King and Parliament both rest safely and solidly upon the will of the people expressed by free and fair election on the basis of universal suffrage. Thus the system has long worked harmoniously, both in peace and in war.
>
> (15 May 1945)

In the 1950s André Mathiot, in his French study of British politics, described the British system as 'an enviable model of democratic government', while adding: 'One can only regret that it could not possibly be transplanted to any other country.' In their classic comparative study of democracies published in 1963, the American political scientists Almond and Verba identified Britain as the exemplar of a successful 'civic culture'. Then, finally, there is the contemporary political scientist Richard Rose, who introduced his textbook on the politics of England (yes, England) with the observation that: 'just as Alexis de Tocqueville travelled to America in 1831 to seek the secrets of democracy, so one might journey to England to seek the secrets of stable, representative government'.

It is not difficult to see why the 'British model' (as it sometimes came to be called) acquired this status. After all, compared with most other societies in Europe, Britain has enjoyed a long and remarkable history of political stability in modern times. Just to take the last hundred years, while countries like France and Germany were regularly making and unmaking their political systems under the impact of war, occupation, extremism, violence, revolution and tyranny, Britain stayed firmly on the path of parliamentary democracy. This was a remarkable achievement, especially in the turbulent circumstances of the first half of the

1. 'envied and enviable . . .': Winston Churchill eulogizes Britain's political system (1945)

20th century. It merited a proper amount of self-congratulation, except from those who wanted to bring the house down.

But, as ever, there is more to be said about the Britishness of British politics than this kind of comfortable summary allows for. Up until the time of the French Revolution at the end of the 18th century, it was Britain's revolutionary history that defined its political tradition; and 'the British had a European reputation, whether admired or abhorred, as a politically volatile people given to regicide and rebellion' (Lively and Lively, *Democracy in Britain: A Reader*). In the 17th century Britain was a pretty bloody place. Nor has the modern period been without its share of turbulence and upheaval, at some moments acutely so. Indeed, in the 1970s the British model ceased to be the object of envy and emulation and came to be seen as the European basket case, the home of an adversarial kind of politics that prevented effective policy-making and brought the country to its knees. 'One does not have to be a doom-monger', wrote the political scientist Anthony King in 1975, 'to sense that something is wrong with our polity as well as our economy'. This is a reminder of a larger point, that political stability of the British kind is not the same as policy success, as the post-war British economic record makes clear. The lines of connection, and disconnection, in this area are much more complex.

Then there is the Irish Question, often conveniently forgotten when the eulogies to the British polity are being composed, which has periodically brought violence and terror into a political system celebrated for its orderly continuities. From the beginning of the modern troubles in Northern Ireland in the late 1960s until the end of the 20th century, a citizen of Northern Ireland was over 200 times more likely to die from sectarian violence than a citizen of India, a chilling reminder that a very different kind of political substance is lodged within the famously well-functioning bloodstream of the British body politic. Northern Ireland is the standing exception to any generalization about modern British politics, which is why it has often been dropped from the picture altogether—until it has exploded its way in again—and why the peace process and power-sharing rooted in the historic Good Friday Agreement of 1998 still remains a work in progress.

This is just the most glaring example of a more general tendency among the British not to know about, or care about, who they are. In part, at least, this is the luxury available to a settled people. It can also be myopia, or worse. The English have always been the worst offenders, feeling no need to look beyond the end of their comfortable noses at the nature of the multinational state of which they are the overwhelmingly dominant part. This is why they have had trouble in coming to terms with devolution and have shown no desire to embrace it for themselves. But the tendency is a general one. The terms 'England' and 'Britain', and 'Great Britain' and 'United Kingdom', are constantly used and misused by people who have no idea what they mean or how they are different, or what their historical provenance is. There can scarcely have been a state in which its citizens were so hopelessly muddled about where they lived.

As the historian Norman Davies puts it, in his epic account of *The Isles*:

> One of the most extraordinary aspects of the current scene lies in the number of citizens of the United Kingdom who do not appear to be familiar with the basic parameters of the state in which they live. They often do not know what it is called; they do not distinguish between the whole and the constituent parts; and they have never grasped the most elementary facts of its development. Confusion reigns on every hand.

A good example is accidentally provided by the American writer, Bill Bryson, in his best-selling account of his journeying around Britain. Searching for the grave of George Orwell in Nuneham Courtenay cemetery in Oxfordshire, he comes upon the grave of

Asquith, who had been prime minister at the height of the British Empire in the early 20th century. Bryson is surprised that the inscription on the headstone describes Asquith as having been prime minister of *England*. He should not have been surprised. This is entirely typical of the prevailing confusions and elisions. The opening sentence of D. L. Keir's standard work on *The Constitutional History of Modern Britain* reads: 'Continuity has been the dominant characteristic in the development of English government'. He might have added that confusion has been the dominant characteristic in descriptions of the British polity.

Yet the confusion is the reality. It can seem merely pedantic to try to hang on to some proper distinctions and definitions. That Britain is not an island. That England (the part) is not Britain (the whole). That 'Great Britain' refers to England, Scotland and Wales, the single kingdom created by the Treaty of Union between England and Scotland in 1707. That the 'United Kingdom' refers to the United Kingdom of Great Britain and Northern Ireland, established in 1921 and ending the 1801 union of Great Britain with Ireland (the former United Kingdom). Although the state has undergone major structural transformations since 1707, in 1801 and 1921, the catch-all term 'British' that was invented in the 18th century has endured. It may be a word in search of a definition, but in its imprecision it has also been characteristically British.

The style guide produced by the *Guardian* newspaper for its journalists offers an example of an interesting attempt to traverse this conceptual bog. Here is an extract from it:

> *Britain/UK*: These terms are synonymous, despite what you might have been told. Britain is the official short form of United Kingdom of Great Britain and Northern Ireland. Used as adjectives, therefore, British and UK mean the same. Great Britain, however, refers only to the mainland of England, Wales and Scotland.

Great Britain: England, Wales and Scotland. If you want to include Northern Ireland, use Britain or UK.

England: Take care not to offend by saying England or English when you mean Britain or British.

Along with its further advice on how to negotiate the linguistic and political minefields associated with 'Ulster' and 'Ireland', this probably takes us just about as far as we can usefully go on this front. It is quite enough to show that the Britishness of British politics comes laden with ambiguities. These have recently had to be confronted as devolution has unpacked one version of the United Kingdom and replaced it with another, but old habits nevertheless die hard.

Old habits are also the product of long experience. The identification of ambiguities and confusions in the British political experience should not be allowed to obscure those distinctive features which have given the political system its underlying shape and form. Many of these are buried deep in history, geography, culture, and social structure. The question of what causes what (for example, is Britain's long history of political stability a product of its political system or is its stable political system a product of a unified society and an uninterrupted history?) is endlessly asked and perennially unanswered. The truth is that everything connects with everything else, shaping and being shaped in turn. How could it be otherwise? Fortunately, this need not detain us unduly here, except as a preface to logging some of the indispensable shaping factors in the making of British politics.

Many of these are well rehearsed and require little further embellishment. However, this does not diminish their significance, or their continuing impact. The fact of geography that separated Britain from the continental land mass of Europe meant that it was unlikely to be a 'normal' European power. It has had no experience of successful invasion or occupation since 1066.

When the countries of Europe emerged from the Second World War with the belief that the nation state had failed, requiring new pan-European political institutions to be built, Britain believed instead that it had triumphed. It was the nation's 'finest hour', when Britain had 'stood alone'. It is impossible to understand the subsequent history of Britain's troubled relationship with 'Europe' without also understanding the force of these different historical (and geographical) trajectories. It explains why Euroscepticism has been much stronger in Britain than in the rest of the EU; and why Britain has acquired its 'awkward partner' status.

Britain avoided other major ruptures, too; or at least got them out of the way early enough to permit several centuries of orderly political evolution and continuity. Britain knew all about religious strife and struggles over the control of the state, but believed that these had largely been settled by the end of the 17th century. In the modern period (since the French Revolution), although Britain has also felt the force of the battles over nationhood, rights, freedom, democracy, and class that have shaped the modern history of Europe, it avoided an experience of decisive rupture. Without a modern revolutionary moment, Britain was not compelled to remake its political institutions, draw up a new constitution, or decide what kind of state it wanted to be. It just went on being what it was, more or less. This might be seen as a peculiar blessing, or as a kind of curse, but it is a fundamental fact about British politics.

This is usually described in the language of adaptation and flexibility (on which more will be said in the next chapter, on the constitution). It has also been described, less pompously, as Muddling Through, or make-it-up-as-you-go-along politics, or (by Peter Hennessy) as the politics of a Back-of-the-Envelope nation. It is reflected in the visible continuity of the institutional landscape, still in the 21st century with a monarchy and a House of Lords, and in the predilection for not abolishing anything if it can be induced to mutate and evolve. New bits may be added on,

2. Britain, which Britain? A poster in the Second World War supplies one answer

but old bits are rarely taken away. This is why British politics *looks* so familiar, never more so than when the Queen arrives in all Her Majesty to perform the State Opening of Parliament and to read out the Gracious Speech in which she announces what 'my' government and ministers are intending to do. David Cameron spars with Ed Miliband across the two sword-lengths' width of the House of Commons chamber, much as Churchill and Attlee did half a century ago, and Gladstone and Disraeli a century earlier. Even when the reality has changed, the outward appearance of British politics looks reassuringly the same.

It is always difficult to judge, at any single moment, whether a political tradition is changing its underlying character as a consequence of particular events or altered circumstances, or whether its broad continuities are still intact. British politics have regularly been described by commentators over the years as being 'in transition'. It is a question much discussed again now. Constitutional changes are making their impact felt, along with significant shifts in Britain's society, economy, and culture. A succession of recent crises—in Parliament, in finance, and in the media—have rocked institutions and damaged trust. The failure of the 2010 general election to produce a winning majority for any party, for the first time in the country's post-1945 history, signalled a new political environment, just as the prospect of prolonged austerity following the financial crash represented a new economic environment. We shall have to return to what all this means for British politics in the final chapter. One thing is certain: it is much easier to identify what the 'Britishness' of British politics has consisted of in the past than what it might consist of now or in the future.

For example, an old examination question on British politics courses used to ask students to discuss Balfour's remark about the British being 'a people so fundamentally at one that they can safely afford to bicker'. This seemed to be a truisim about the British political culture, an expression of a fundamental unity that transcended differences and so enabled the political system to achieve a stable continuity. Of course, it was never quite as simple as that, but it does nevertheless identify a crucial feature of the British political experience. George Orwell put his finger on this in the 1940s when he described how 'the proletariat of Hammersmith will not arise and massacre the bourgeoisie of Kensington: they are not different enough'. Britain (and England in particular) was exceptionally marked by its class divisions. 'The English were the only European people who sorted themselves out by class at mealtimes', observed A. J. P. Taylor: 'the masses took their principal meal at midday, their betters in the evening'. But Britain was also marked by the extent of its overarching social unity. Reform, not revolution, was the watchword. Parliament, not the barricades, was the route of advance.

This unity was helped by the empire, a profoundly 'British' experience in which all could share. It brought the separate nations and classes of Britain under its generous wing, as people learnt to paint the world red. That is why the retreat from empire—memorably captured in US Secretary of State Dean Acheson's remark in 1962 that 'Great Britain has lost an Empire and has not yet found a role'—produced prolonged policy agonizing about the country's place in the world. The common experience of war, especially the two great conflicts of the 20th century, further strengthened social unity. It was also helped by the particular nature of the demand for welfare and social justice, which framed itself in class rather than territorial terms (joining Clydeside with the Rhondda, Cockneys with Geordies), looked for 'British' solutions of the kind exemplified by the 'national' health service and found in the British Labour Party a political instrument that gave it a local idiom and integrated it into established constitutional procedures and institutions. This is a bald summary of a rich history, but it is an indispensable part of any understanding of British politics.

It is not that Britain lacks differences. These remain sharp and marked—of class, ethnicity, culture, generation, region, nation, religion, and much else—and some grow sharper; new issues appear as old ones subside; and traditional attitudes (such as deference, trust, and duty) are replaced by a sceptical questioning of authority and even a willingness to kick over the traces at times. The fragmentation of a traditional class structure has brought with it a political fragmentation. All this demands caution in making generalizations. Yet it has undoubtedly been the case, and remains so to a significant extent, that the commonality of British society has given a particular character to its politics. It has not been necessary (at least not until recently, and always with Northern Ireland as the standing exception) to structure political life around religious, ethnic, or territorial divisions, as it has often been necessary to do elsewhere. Nor is there the regionalization of political life that is common in much of Europe, with proud provincial capitals and strong regional newspapers. In Britain all political roads have traditionally led to London. People have overwhelmingly read the same newspapers, watched the same television programmes, and participated in the same 'national' conversation (with the BBC as a core British institution). The post-devolution row over whether the BBC's six o'clock news bulletin should be British or Scottish brought this contested commonality into sharp relief, while devolution itself was just one indication among others that a more differentiated society would involve important consequences for the political system.

The old building blocks of Britishness may now be weakening (and in need of replacement or reinvention). The legacy of empire has produced a population that is much more diverse, giving rise to arguments about the relationship between Britishness and multiculturalism—with David Cameron attacking 'state multiculturalism' in a speech in 2011 and identifying it as contributing factor to extremism and Islamic terrorism—while immigration has become a potent and often toxic political issue. At the same time, devolution strengthened separate identities and threatened to take Britain apart. Perhaps this is why the popular celebration of the Queen's Diamond Jubilee in 2012, followed by national pride in the success of 'Team GB' in the London Olympics of that year, could feel to many like a badly needed reaffirmation of a Britishness that had become much less sure of itself than it had been sixty years earlier.

But that is to run ahead. Speculation about where British politics might be going has to wait until we have established where it has come from, and how its essential character has been formed. What is this essential character? It has been distinguished by a striking simplicity. This can be a shock to the system for those accustomed to more elaborately ordered political arrangements elsewhere. Raymond Seitz, a recent American ambassador to Britain, describes (in his *Over Here*) what it was like to leave the tortuous legislative process of Washington and arrive in the brutal simplicities of Westminster:

Coming from this kind of fractured, fractious federal background, an American arrives on British shores astonished to discover how unfettered a modern British government is. When I first lived here, in the mid-1970s, it took me a long time to understand that a British government, with a simple majority in the House of Commons, can do pretty much what it wants to. If the party in power can count on having one more warm body in its lobby than all the other bodies combined in the other lobby, there is nothing to prevent the government having its way. I kept looking for constitutional checks and institutional balances that could stay the will of a British government. But I could find none. In face of such arbitrary omnipotence, I could suddenly imagine myself as an American revolutionary, grabbing my flintlock from the wall above the fireplace and rushing into the forest to take a few potshots at the Redcoats.

This is often described as the British tradition of 'strong government'. It is said to reflect both a particular history and the temper of a people. It was forged out of a state that had early on established a centralized grip on its territory, earlier and tighter than elsewhere. Even though monarchs had to learn to govern with the 'consent' of representatives, eventually having to settle for a Crown-in-Parliament arrangement that concealed a fundamental shift in the balance of power, what remained intact was a governing tradition. The identity of those doing the governing may have altered, but the activity of governing remained remarkably unchanged. The arrival of democratic politics did little to disturb this tradition, perhaps even strengthening it by endowing it with an enhanced legitimacy. It was a governing arrangement that was top–down rather than bottom–up. Power was centralized and concentrated. It enabled governments to govern, or so it was said.

It was also a very British arrangement, in its governing simplicity. Government was a craft, not an artefact. It required not elaborate books of rules but a proper apprenticeship. It could be entrusted to good chaps who could be relied upon to play the game. There need be no nonsense about the sovereignty of the people or the fundamental rights of citizens. The rule of law, grounded in the common law tradition and the independence of the judiciary, was the protector of liberty. A doctrine of representation was developed which guaranteed a safe distance between the governors and the governed. The governed seemed content to be governed in this way, as long as they had the periodic opportunity to kick one lot of governors out and put another lot in. Those who ran the state, whether as politicians, administrators, policemen, or judges, were not regarded as corrupt (as it was said of Sir Hector Rose, the Permanent Secretary in C. P. Snow's novel *The New Men*, 'it was absurd to suppose that Rose could be bought by any money under Heaven: it would be like trying to slip Robespierre a five-pound note') and it was therefore reasonable to let them get on with it.

If pushed too far such a portrait becomes a caricature, while some of its features are clearly changing. Yet it does still capture much of the essential character of the British political tradition. This is why it is necessary to add some qualifications to those descriptions of the stable, representative democracy of the 'British model' that were cited at the beginning of this chapter. To many Britain has seemed a funny, and reluctant, kind of democracy. This is what R. H. Tawney meant when he described Britain as having accepted democracy

> as a convenience, like an improved system of telephones; she did not dedicate herself to it as the expression of a moral idea of comradeship and equality, the avowal of which would leave nothing the same. She changed her political garments, but not her heart. She carried into the democratic era, not only the institutions, but the social habits and mentality of the oldest and toughest plutocracy in the world…she went to the ballot box touching her hat.

There had been suspicion, and fear, among the old governing classes about what democracy might bring with it, as the untutored masses staked their political claims, and much relief as it was safely domesticated by established governing traditions. It did not demand the wholesale reorganization of the political system on democratic first principles, nor did it seek to circumscribe those who governed with a new set of democratic accountabilities. Rather, political life went on pretty much as before. When Lord John Russell had steered the Great Reform Act of 1832 through Parliament, often seen as the British alternative to continental revolution, he dismissed fears about the arrival of democracy and 'denied altogether that the measure would have the effect of rendering the House a democratic assemblage in that sense of the word'.

What remained intact, above all else, was a strong executive centre. This was further strengthened, rather than constrained, by the arrival of democratic politics, as majority parties claimed their right to the full resources of the state without hindrance or interference. As the state grew in size and scope, a governing tradition that secured unhindered enjoyment of it was a very considerable asset indeed. All that was needed to receive its blessings was a parliamentary majority. Once in secure possession of this, the governing landscape was remarkably free of institutional blockages or impediments. There was no separation of powers to create alternative centres of authority. There were no meddling judges to tell you that what you were doing was unconstitutional. There was no constitutional rule-book to define the parameters of your power. You could, in short, do what you could get away with.

It is no wonder, then, that foreign observers have been struck by the governing simplicities of the British system, or that foreign politicians have often salivated at the governing resources available to their British equivalents. A British prime minister, especially one with a united party and a secure parliamentary majority, is a far more powerful figure than an American president. Yet this governing capacity has come at a price in terms of accountability. It is a price that the British people, at least until quite recently, have seemed more than willing to pay. The journalist Hugo Young put it like this:

> Contrary to popular myth, and to the incantations of political leaders who can hardly afford to give the question serious study, the British do not passionately care about democracy. As long as they get a vote every few years and the children don't starve, they are prepared to put up with almost anything politicians throw at them. They do not have the habit of making life difficult for government, especially a strong government. They are prepared to be quiet accessories to mandates they never really gave. This preference, which is for strong government over accountable government, is to be found throughout the British parliamentary system.
> (*Guardian*, 15 September 1988)

We shall have to consider whether it is still possible, in the early part of the 21st century—with stronger accountabilities, new constraints, disappearing majorities—to characterize British politics in this way. Much is certainly changing, in both attitudes and institutions, but much also stays the same. There are plenty of new clothes, but is there a new body? It is surely difficult to talk about a 'British model' as the elixir of stable, representative democracy, when it is a model so clearly rooted in the peculiarities of the British political tradition, itself rooted in a particular history and society. This has led some to talk of a 'British exceptionalism' instead, which is clearly not for borrowing. Yet it may be that Britain is currently in the process of becoming less exceptional. An example of this is the recent attention to constitutional matters, and it is to the constitution that we turn next.

Chapter 2
The constitution: old and new

What of Magna Carta? Did she die in vain?

(Tony Hancock)

Soon after the 1992 general election, when I had managed by a whisker to get myself elected as a Member of Parliament, there was an almighty political row about the Conservative government's decision to close down most of the country's coal mines. I had a pit in my constituency, and so was much engaged by the issue. When my local pit was added to the closure list, not having been on it previously, I was furious. This produced a moment which still makes me cringe with embarrassment as I recall it, but which also offers a useful point of entry for thinking about the nature of the constitution in Britain.

The President of the Board of Trade, Michael Heseltine (who liked to be called The President), was making a statement about the pit closures to a packed and noisy House of Commons. He was constantly interrupted by Labour MPs who wanted his blood for what he was doing to the communities they represented. When he refused to take any more interventions, I stood up and shouted 'Point of order!' This is a common parliamentary tactic for getting yourself heard, as it causes the Speaker to halt proceedings so that the invariably bogus point of order can be taken. As the House stilled, I told the Speaker I wanted to raise a 'constitutional point of order' and proceeded to mutter something about the convention for ministers to 'consider their position' (code for 'resign') if their policies collapsed or if previous positions had to be reversed. I realized at once that the bearpit that is the House of Commons is not the place for such arcane constitutional niceties. This was confirmed by the Speaker's contemptuous dismissal of my intervention with some words about 'not knowing anything about constitutions here'.

That is precisely the point. We do not know anything about constitutions here, at least not in the sense that they are known about elsewhere. We are not even familiar with the basic language of constitutional debate. The British enjoy a marvellous constitutional illiteracy. They think pluralism is a lung disease. This is not because they have no constitution (as famously alleged by Alexis de Tocqueville in his *Democracy in America* (1835) and variously repeated ever since), but because they have had a constitution of a peculiar kind. Above all else it has been a political constitution, shaped and reshaped by changing political circumstances and so forever on the move. This makes it peculiarly difficult to pin down. Some regard this as a grave disability, others as a rich blessing.

Constitutions are rules of the political game, or at least the most important ones. They tell you how the game should be played. Usually there is a book of rules, as in other games, so that it is easy to check whether the game is being played properly. This also provides something to wave in the face of cheats. Yet it may impose a straitjacket too, preventing the game's natural evolution and development in response to new players and changed circumstances. Further, even where there is a book of rules, it may not accurately describe how the game is actually played. Britain is rare among democratic states (only Israel and New Zealand belong to the same category) in not having a book of constitutional rules. There are lots of rules that are written down though, from ancient statutes such as the Bill of Rights of 1689 and the Act of Settlement of 1701 to very recent legislation on human rights, devolution, freedom of information, and party funding. If all this constitutional legislation was brought together, it would make a vast and impressive volume. Indeed, following the 2010 general election, some of it was brought together by the Cabinet Secretary in *The Cabinet Manual*, described as 'a guide to laws, conventions and rules on the operation of government'.

This is why it has always been misleading to describe Britain as having an unwritten constitution, or no proper constitution at all. Rather it has a constitution that is not codified or enacted into a single book of rules. It is a great accumulated jumble of statutes, common law provisions and precedents, conventions and guidebooks. As such it is an awesome mess, horrifying to constitutional purists but an authentic expression of a particular history. It is a political constitution, but also a historical one. The constitutional shed is crammed full of all the objects collected over a long political lifetime. Nobody is quite sure which still work, or whether some have been superseded by others, even as more objects are squeezed in. From time to time someone (a Bagehot or a Dicey) tries to describe the contents in a coherent and intelligible way, although this description may differ somewhat from the last time it was attempted. Occasionally it is suggested (most recently by Gordon Brown, prime minister from 2007 to 2010, who floated the idea of a written constitution) that the shed should be sorted out once and for all, and everything put into a proper order, but this has always seemed a much too daunting task and the need has never been sufficiently pressing. If more room was needed, then it was easier just to add on an extension.

The vindication of such arrangements, or so it was traditionally argued, was that they worked. 'We Englishmen are Very Proud of our Constitution, Sir', declared Dickens's Mr Podsnap: 'It was Bestowed Upon Us by Providence. No Other Country is so Favoured as This Country.' In its combination of liberty with order, and in its protections against arbitrary government, the British constitution seemed to offer lessons to the world. Certainly this was widely believed in the 18th century, as the 'matchless constitution' that had been bequeathed by the Glorious Revolution of 1688 was celebrated at home and admired from abroad. Parliament had disciplined royal power, the independence of judges had been safeguarded, and the resulting system of intrinsic checks and balances could be presented as the exemplar of a proper constitutionalism. The 'true excellence' of this form of government, according to Blackstone's *Commentaries on the Laws of England* (1765–9), was that 'all the parts of it form a mutual check upon each other'.

The idea of balance was held to be fundamental, producing a practical form of 'mixed' government that prevented tyranny while enabling effectiveness. The growing dominance of the Commons was balanced by the influence of the Crown and the Lords, thus securing a constitutional equilibrium. 'It is by this mixture of monarchical, aristocratical and democratical power, blended together in one system, and by these three estates balancing one another, that our free constitution has been preserved so long inviolate', declared another 18th-century constitutional theorist Henry St John Bolingbroke, adding: 'It secures society against the miseries which are inseparable from simple forms of government, and is as liable as little as possible to the inconveniences that arise in mixed forms.' Alongside these ideas of balance and mixture was the concept of a separation of powers (between executive, legislative, and judicial functions) as an axial constitutional principle. In his *The Spirit of the Laws* (1748), Montesquieu famously translated what he believed to be the model of such an admirable and ingenious separation in Britain into a more general constitutional formula that was to be influential with those (like the American founding fathers) seeking to construct constitutions on the basis of sound principles.

There is a good deal of irony in all of this, since the British system has since come to be characterized as peculiarly lacking in institutional checks and balances and with the principle of a separation of powers conspicuous by its absence, at least in any pure form. These were really no more than descriptions and interpretations of a historical constitution at certain moments in its development, heavily influenced in many cases by the political predilections of the commentators themselves, rather than accounts of securely anchored constitutional principles. Yet they have been, and remain, influential in shaping beliefs about the constitution. The traditional notion of a constitutional balance between Crown, Lords, and Commons is still captured by the reference to the 'Crown-in-Parliament' as the formal source of legislative authority. Even today every law passed by Parliament begins with these words: 'Be it enacted by the Queen's most Excellent Majesty, by and with the advice and consent of the Lords Spiritual and Temporal, and Commons, in this present Parliament assembled, and by the authority of the same...'.

Note how 'and Commons' just sneaks in to this august assemblage. This is the moment to summon up the ghost of Walter Bagehot, whose celebrated account of *The English Constitution* (1867) sought to strip away the appearance from the reality, the 'dignified' from the 'efficient'. Like so many anxious 19th-century minds, Bagehot wanted to know how the pressures from an advancing democracy could be contained within the parameters of an ancient constitution. He found the answer in an elaborate system of smoke and mirrors. The 'dignified' constitution (in which the monarchy played a crucial role) would continue to provide a focus for the 'vacant many', while the 'efficient' constitution passed into the hands of a middle-class House of Commons and the Cabinet ('a combining committee—a hyphen which joins, a buckle which fastens, the legislative part of the State to the executive part of the State') now provided the mechanism to keep the governing show on the road. It was a striking portrait, with the efficient secret of the constitution no longer located in the separation of powers but in their fusion. The nature of the governing mixture had changed.

3. The 'balanced' constitution of King, Lords, and Commons is represented in this 18th-century engraving

Yet there remained a real conundrum once traditional accounts of a balanced constitution were abandoned, as they had to be once the dominance of the Commons was underwritten by an advancing democracy. The conundrum turned on the principle of parliamentary sovereignty, long enshrined as the organizing principle of legislative authority in Britain, and how it could be reconciled with an old system of checks and balances once power was fused and a parliamentary majority could deploy it to secure its unhindered way. If parliamentary sovereignty meant that Parliament could do anything it liked, and if this sovereignty was now effectively exercised by the Commons alone (once the 1911 Parliament Act had put the Lords in its place), and if the Commons was now in the iron grip of the executive (courtesy of the rigid party system), where did this leave the constitution? Where were the checks and balances? Where was the protection against arbitrary government? Where were the limits of the state?

Such questions have become central to modern constitutional (and political) argument in Britain, but they were already surfacing at the end of the 19th century when A. V. Dicey's classic interpretation of the constitution appeared (*Introduction to the Study of the Law of the Constitution*, 1885). This is relevant here, since its purpose was to navigate an old constitution into a new democratic legitimacy. If the sovereignty of Parliament ('the right to make or unmake any law whatever') was the 'one fundamental law of the British Constitution', how was this to be reconciled with the fundamental democratic principle of the sovereign people? What was there to prevent a sovereign Parliament exercising arbitrary power over a sovereign people?

These were Dicey's questions, just as they remain ours. His answer rejected any resort to the formal rigidities of constitutions elsewhere, which were inferior in every respect to 'the most flexible polity in existence', anchored in the rule of law and conventional understandings. The reason why the legal sovereignty of Parliament could not in practice lead to arbitrary government, despite the theoretical possibility, was that it was now firmly rooted in the political sovereignty of the electorate. A parliamentary majority would only do what a majority of the people wanted. Legal sovereignty and political sovereignty went hand in hand, such that 'our modern code of constitutional morality secures, though in a roundabout way, what is called abroad the "sovereignty of the people"'. The circle was squared, and the constitution had been safely navigated—without the need for radical overhaul—into new democratic waters.

But had it really? Even Dicey came to doubt it, once he switched role from academic jurist to Liberal Unionist partisan. In the former role he demonstrated why a sovereign Parliament would always serve the wishes of a sovereign people; in the latter role he denounced it for failing to do so. This Dicey wanted to know how a transient Commons majority could 'arrogate to itself that legislative omnipotence which of right belongs to the nation' and warned (the context was the 1911 Parliament Act) that 'no country, except England, now dreams of placing itself under the rule of a single elected House'. He therefore looked to the referendum as a protective constitutional device ('a democratic check on democratic evils') against the misuse of parliamentary sovereignty by temporary majorities. It is not necessary to share Dicey's politics, or to agree with his remedy, to think that he was on to something.

These sorts of arguments were not to be heard again until much later in the 20th century, after a long period of intervening calm on the constitutional front. The 20th century was the era when disciplined party government really came into its own, with its legitimating armoury of mandates and manifestos, and a constitution which enabled a majority party to deploy parliamentary sovereignty without check or hindrance proved especially congenial to its governing purposes. The idea that the legal sovereignty of Parliament merely reflected the political sovereignty of the people, and that this was the end of the argument as far as democracy was concerned, was a brutally simple and compelling constitutional perspective. It really required no further discussion, and for a long period received none.

What it produced (and justified) was a constitution in which power was highly concentrated, where the prerogatives of the Crown had become the powers of the executive, and where formal constraints on that power were notable by their absence. In international terms, Britain was out on a limb. There was no book of constitutional rules; no supreme court to guard the constitution against the politicians; no charter of citizens' rights that had to be complied with; no other tiers of government that enjoyed constitutional status and protection; no second chamber with power to rival the first; and no electoral system that enforced proportionality between votes cast and seats won. This was a 'winner-takes-all' system with a vengeance, not just in terms of how the first-past-the-post electoral system worked but in terms of the governing resources available to a winning party. Getting your hands on the great prize of government, with all its unconstrained power, conditioned everything. The style and culture of political life, with its ferocious adversarialism and yah-boo polarities, both reflected and reinforced the essential nature of this system.

It was a system in which it was difficult to say what was 'unconstitutional' at any particular moment, or by whom this could be said with any authority. It was also a system in which 'constitutional' laws had no special status or recognition, and were not subject to any separate procedure in their making, unmaking, or amending. When the House of Commons passes a piece of constitutional legislation it does not identify it as such or apply distinctive procedures to its consideration or extra conditions to its approval. Constitutional laws are simply ordinary laws with a constitutional subject matter. Nor can they be entrenched in any formal way, since a sovereign Parliament can make or unmake any law whatsoever, including laws about the constitution. For example, the law passed by the Cameron government after the 2010 election providing for a referendum before any further powers are transferred to the EU has constitutional force only for as long as it is politically acceptable. This is why it could be said with authority in the House of Commons that nothing was known about constitutions there. It is also why, far more than the absence of a codified book of rules, Britain has sometimes been thought not to have a constitution at all.

The 'constitutional' laws passed in the early part of the 20th century had set the framework for political life for 50 years afterwards, without any serious challenge or controversy. The ascendancy of the Commons over the Lords, and therefore of the executive over the political system, had been finally established in the 1911 Parliament Act (with a further tightening in 1949). The final triumph of universal suffrage was effectively sealed in the 1918 Representation of the People Act (though all women over 21 were not included until 1928). That Britain would remain a unitary state seemed finally established when the prospect of Home Rule for Ireland leading to a quasi-federal 'home rule all round' ended with the 1921 Anglo-Irish Treaty. This represented a spectacular failure of constitutional politics in Britain, neither keeping Ireland in the union nor freeing it completely from it, but it was nevertheless a settlement of a kind.

These measures served to keep the constitution off the political agenda for a large part of the 20th century. Then it began to creep back in, from a number of different directions, until by the end of the century Britain found itself in the thick of a constitutional revolution. What had happened to bring this about? The biggest jolt to the traditional constitution was the one that was least noticed at the time. When Britain joined the Common Market (now European Union) in 1972, it may have believed that it was simply joining an economic club but in fact it was transforming its constitution. In giving primacy to European law over domestic law in the ever-expanding areas where EU law held sway (a position confirmed in pivotal legal judgments in Britain), the old doctrine of parliamentary sovereignty was effectively blown out of the water. Parliament was no longer sovereign, except in the face-saving sense that it could still vote to leave the European Union if it wanted to.

There was much bewilderment, and gnashing of political teeth, in Britain as it was slowly realized what had been done. There were claims that when the British people had voted to confirm the country's membership of 'Europe' in a referendum in 1975, they had been innocent of the constitutional enormity of their decision (and deliberately kept so, in some versions). This produced much railing against 'rule by Brussels' and ensured that the European issue rumbled away in the interstices of British politics, periodically exploding, especially in the Conservative Party. The crisis in the Eurozone has renewed calls for a referendum in Britain, although on what question it is not clear. Yet the significance of EU membership for Britain's constitutional arrangements remains immense and undeniable.

It surfaced in poignant form on 4 July 2001, when a consumer protection officer in Sunderland purchased a bunch of bananas from a greengrocer, Mr Thorburn, who did not have his scales calibrated in metric measures and sold the bananas, as he had always done, per imperial pound. There followed a prosecution which made Mr Thorburn into a *cause célèbre* and generated much popular and political excitement. It was left to the judge in the case to spell out in brutal constitutional terms why Mr Thorburn had to comply with European Union law, as implemented by a parliamentary order, in the matter of how he sold his produce:

> One of the most important reasons to justify European Union is
> that of conformity and uniformity . . . It would destroy the concept
> of the Union if member states could go off on legislative frolics of

their own. . . . From the moment the Right Honourable Edward
Heath signed the Treaty on behalf of the UK he also agreed to the
eventual demise of the imperial system. . . . In 1972 Parliament took
a step which probably no British Parliament before it has
taken . . . This country quite voluntarily surrendered the once
seemingly immortal concept of the sovereignty of parliament and
legislative freedom by membership of the European Union. . . . So
long as this country remains a member of the European Union
then the laws of this country are subject to the doctrine of the
primacy of community law. . . . This country has decided that its
political future lies in Europe . . . As such it has joined this
European club and by so doing has agreed to be bound by the
rules and regulations of the club . . .

So there. The constitutional world had changed for greengrocers,
and for everybody else. But it was changing in other ways too,
unsettling a constitutional settlement that had for long remained
uncontested. The sharper ideological antagonisms of the 1970s
and 1980s threw into relief the nature of a political system which
delivered such unconstrained power to parties which enjoyed
diminishing levels of electoral support. When the Conservative
politician Lord Hailsham, with Labour in his sights, coined the
phrase 'elective dictatorship' in the 1970s to describe the
contemporary constitution, it found a wide resonance. Many
thought that the term received its practical demonstration in the
Conservative governments of Mrs Thatcher after 1979 (in which
Hailsham served), which seemed to display a 'one of us' governing
arrogance and barely concealed contempt for the conventional
rules of the game. This period served to provide a crash course of
constitutional education and helped to promote new attention to
issues of constitutional reform.

More immediate pressures came from the growing demand in
Scotland (and also, less so, in Wales) for serious devolution of
power. The need to respond to this pressure produced an abortive
Royal Commission on the Constitution in the 1970s and failed

referendums, but 20 years later the pressure was even more intense and could no longer be safely contained by the centre. If the union was to be preserved, it clearly had to be reformed. Then, as ever, there was Northern Ireland, which became a constant preoccupation for British governments (if not for the British people, who adopted a despairingly blind eye to the province) once the post-1921 version of self-government broke down and direct rule was reimposed in 1972, requiring endless initiatives in constitutional ingenuity in an effort to find a way of governing that divided community.

What all this meant was that, in the final quarter of the 20th century, the constitution was on the move again. New political pressures (including a developing sense of sleaze and distrust) were demanding a response. A famously flexible constitution was about to be stretched to the limit, perhaps even beyond. The decisive moment came with the election of Tony Blair's Labour government in 1997, with its commitment to a range of sweeping constitutional reforms. For the first time in Britain's modern history the process of constitutional change and adaptation was not to occur merely as a response to events and pressures, but as a deliberately engineered programme of constitutional revolution. As Blair himself had put it in 1996:

> Changing the way we govern, and not just changing our
> government is no longer an optional extra for Britain.... Times have
> changed. Constitutional issues are now at the heart of political
> debate. We gauge that constitutional conservatism is dying and that
> popular support for change is tangible and steadfast.

The constitution would never be the same again, nor intended to be.

The sheer scale of the reform programme was extraordinary, as was the extent to which it was actually delivered and the speed with which this was done. We shall return to it in the final chapter, to assess its durable significance for politics in Britain, but for the moment it is enough to register its sweep and scope. Two measures stand out. The devolution of power to Scotland (vast) and Wales (limited) represented a fundamental break with a traditionally centralized and unitary state. It created new political systems and new political cultures. Then the Human Rights Act (1998), effectively incorporating the European Convention on Human Rights into domestic law, introduced a new judicial benchmark against which actions of public authorities (and Acts of Parliament) have to be tested. Although it did not involve a full-blown constitutional court, nor a power for judges to strike down Acts of Parliament, there is no doubt that the 1998 Human Rights Act has to be set alongside the 1972 European Communities Act in putting a new constitutional framework around British politics.

On all sides the impact of change and reform was felt. Hereditary peers were removed from the House of Lords and a royal commission pointed the way to further reform. Northern Ireland acquired an Assembly that, in its composition and operation, was a triumph of constitutional ingenuity. London acquired a new local authority, with a directly elected mayor, and the internal structure of all local authorities was reorganized. An official inquiry considered and recommended a new voting system for Westminster. Freedom of information legislation challenged a traditional secrecy. Party funding and electoral organization became the province of a new Electoral Commission, which joined a set of constitutional watchdogs. Control over interest rates, and therefore over monetary policy, was transferred from the Treasury to the Monetary Policy Committee of the Bank of England, thus creating a new and independent source of power within the government of Britain. The visible separation of power was strengthened as judges moved from the House of Lords into a new Supreme Court. New kinds of electoral systems sprouted all over the place, and referendums became the established vehicles for approving constitutional change.

1. Reforming the machine (*Economist*, 18 April 1998)

Merely to recite such a catalogue of reform between 1997 and 2010 is enough to register its significance for British politics. It made it possible, and plausible, to announce (as did Anthony King, in his 2001 Hamlyn Lectures *Does the United Kingdom Still have a Constitution?*) that 'the traditional British constitution . . . is dead'. If so, it was not clear what kind of new constitution had been born. Much had changed, but much had also stayed the same. There may have been a constitutional revolution, but there had been no grand design behind it and no concerted attempt to make its constituent elements fit together into a coherent whole. Yet it had unleashed a constitutional dynamic that would bring enduring (and unpredictable) consequences for British politics.

One consequence was a developing tension between politicians and judges on the matter of human rights (especially in relation to terrorist suspects). There seemed to be a conflict between two constitutional principles: the sovereignty of Parliament and the rule of law. Who should decide—the judges or the politicians? As Tom Bingham, who had been the country's top judge, observed in his luminous *The Rule of Law*: 'The British people have not repelled the extraneous power of the papacy in spiritual matters and the pretensions of royal power in temporal in order to subject themselves to the unchallengeable rulings of unelected judges'. A way had to be found to manage the potential for tension in the new relationship. Meanwhile, the Conservative-led coalition formed in 2010 set about exploring whether a home-grown 'British' bill of rights would help to get the relationship into better balance.

A further consequence of constitutional change was the momentum it gave to the process of devolution. This had been designed to preserve the union; but it now threatened to destroy it. In 2011 the Nationalists moved from minority to majority rule in Scotland and set a 2014 date for a referendum on independence. The future of the British state itself was now in question. It opened up debate about identities and loyalties of a kind that Britain had not experienced in its modern history. Even the English started asking questions about their own identity and how it might find political expression. If Britain was to continue to exist, it would be because enough people in enough places had decided that they wanted it to. It would also be very different from the unitary state of old.

Even after Labour's constitutional revolution, the coalition government had constitutional ambitions of its own. Liberal Democrat leader Nick Clegg, now deputy prime minister, even promised the biggest reform of British democracy 'since 1832'. In the event a referendum on changing the electoral system to the Alternative Vote was decisively lost in 2011; and another proposal to reform the House of Lords by introducing elections was undermined by Conservative opposition and met the fate of similar proposals made under the previous Labour government. However legislation on fixed-term parliaments was introduced, significantly affecting the power of dissolution; while a massive exercise in parliamentary boundary revision (only failing when Liberal Democrats decided to oppose it in retaliation for Conservative opposition to Lords reform) was designed to reduce the number of MPs and even out the size of constituencies.

Where did all this leave the old political constitution in the second decade of the twenty-first century? The short answer was that it was dead and buried, although it was less clear what it had been replaced by. Where there had once been such simplicity, there was now complexity. Where there had been a clear and unrestricted line of governing authority, there was now a whole array of checks and constraints. Power that had been concentrated was now divided up. What had once been decided politically was now decided by codes, rules, laws, and commissions. The sovereignty of Parliament was eroded; the separation of powers enhanced. In the words of Vernon Bogdanor (in his *The New British Constitution*) this represented 'the beginning of the transformation of Britain into a constitutional state'.

It also made governing a lot more difficult (even before the arrival of coalition politics). From activist judges to devolved parliaments, and from a more confident House of Lords to a less compliant

House of Commons, governments had many more hurdles to get across. Yet the twentieth-century charge had been that government had become too easy and unrestrained; and that a political constitution needed to be constitutionalized. This had now happened. In some ways it was a return, in a different context, to those eighteenth-century descriptions of a mixed constitution with its deliberate checks and balances. An old political constitution might have gone; but only to be replaced by an even older one.

Chapter 3
Arguing: the political conversation

> Never, never underestimate the importance or the power of the tide
> of ideas. No British government has ever been defeated unless and
> until the tide of ideas has turned against it.
>
> (Nigel Lawson, 14 May 1987)

> He was always striving to transmute the small change of politics
> into large principles.
>
> (Michael Foot, on Aneurin Bevan)

Clement Attlee was not a great conversationalist (although he was
a great prime minister, in Labour's reforming administration after
1945). It was once said of him that he would never use one word
when none would do. An expansive sentence might run to 'quite'.
Interviewing him could be tough work, as on this occasion at the
start of the 1951 general election campaign:

INTERVIEWER: Tell us something on how you view the election
prospects.

ATTLEE: Oh, we shall go in with a good fight. Very good. Very good
chance of winning if we go in competently. We always do.

INTERVIEWER: On what will Labour take its stand?

ATTLEE: Well, that's what we shall be announcing shortly.

INTERVIEWER: What are your immediate plans Mr Attlee?

ATTLEE: My immediate plans are to go down to a committee to decide on just that thing as soon as I can get away from here.

INTERVIEWER: Is there anything else you'd like to say about the coming election?

ATTLEE: No.

Now jump ahead half a century, to the world of round-the-clock news fed by the new political industry of soundbite and spin. It is nicely captured by the *Guardian*'s parliamentary sketchwriter, Simon Hoggart, after one Prime Minister's Questions in 1997:

Here's what it's like these days. I returned to our tiny *Guardian* office in Westminster to find three – count them, three – Liberal Democrat spin doctors clustered around.

They were like ants at a picnic. You'd leave one at the door, and find another waiting by your computer screen. As soon as you'd dealt with him, another would turn up over your shoulder.

'Did you like Paddy's intervention?' asked one. 'Wasn't he funny?'

'Jackie Ballard was terrific, wasn't she', said another. 'She was so poised!'

'Look, here's a copy of what Blair actually said last year', said a third, and there was a photocopy of Hansard, proving beyond doubt that, as Leader of the Opposition, Mr Blair has described as mere 'sticking plaster', a sum of money larger than his own government proposes to spend on the NHS.

Don't misunderstand me. All those three spin doctors are intelligent, thoughtful, well-informed young persons. It's a pleasure to do business with them. Their party should pay them huge sums of money.

But you have to wonder about the state of British politics, in which there is such an obsessional concern about these tiny soundbites from the smallest of the three main parties.

This really is how it is now. Clement Attlee would not last for five minutes. Walking the media route between Commons and Millbank one evening, I overheard a couple of earnest young spinners (of unidentified party) discussing their day's work. 'I just wish', said one, 'that we had gone the extra mile'. 'Yes', replied the other, 'I think we might have got GMTV'. This is where, and how, politics takes place now. Politicians trail each other around the television and radio studios, honing and repeating the phrases they have rehearsed, while their hired hands work the press and prepare the ammunition. The voracious appetite of the media demands non-stop feeding and prefers titillating bite-sized morsels that are easily digested to anything more substantial. Politics has become a permanent election campaign, involving an unceasing war of position between the parties, and between the parties and the media.

Because politics is now conducted like this, it becomes harder to see the big picture. Politics needs argument, but when everything is argued about it can be difficult to distinguish real arguments from synthetic ones and significant issues from trivial ones. The tendency for the media to be interested only in arguments as 'splits' (a tendency reinforced further by the post-2010 politics of coalition) adds to the difficulty. For their part politicians seek constantly to construct an overarching 'narrative' of events (as in 'we are having to deal with the debt crisis left by the last government' versus 'this is a recession made in Downing Street') which compresses arguments into neat presentational packages.

Perhaps it is easier for politics to be conducted in this way in an age when ideological antagonisms have become blunted. If political argument is no longer about fundamentals, then presentational politics can provide a substitute for ideological politics. But that is to run ahead. The essential point, to which all this is merely a preamble, is that if a political tradition is to be understood then it is necessary to know what it argues about. Therefore it is only by listening in to Britain's continuing political conversation that we can discover, as with all conversations, what matters to the participants. It is only possible to hear snatches of this conversation here, but enough to get a flavour of what is going on.

Let us start with our old friends 'left' and 'right'. Much of the British political conversation during the past century has been framed by these terms. They have their origin in the French Revolution, and have shaped the political experience of Europe (and beyond) for much of the time since then. They have marked off reformers from reactionaries, liberals from conservatives, and socialists from capitalists. Liberals value individual liberty and limited government; conservatives emphasize traditional authority and social order. Socialists embrace collective action for social justice and the common good; capitalists espouse market freedom for enterprise and efficiency. Here, in a nutshell, is the terrain upon which much political argument in the West has been conducted for the last two centuries, in different modulations and idioms. It has been a running argument between versions of liberty, equality, and order, and between what the state (on behalf of an idea of community) should properly do and what should be left to individual action and preference. Parties and classes have organized themselves around the ideological formulations constructed out of these arguments.

How does Britain fit into this general picture? 'The dialectic between the growing pressures of collectivism and the opposing libertarian tendency is the one supreme fact of our domestic political life as this has developed over the past century and a half': so begins a leading account of British political ideology (W. H. Greenleaf's volume on *The Ideological Heritage* (1983), part of his larger study of the British political tradition). Well, yes and no. Perhaps that is what 'dialectic' means here. Although the growth of state provision, under the pressure of democratic forces, is certainly a central fact of Britain's modern history, how this was played out in practice is more complicated and mixed up than the notion of 'opposing tendencies' suggests and reflects distinctive features of the British political tradition.

For Britain had a peculiar 'left' and a peculiar 'right'. British socialism stood outside the tradition of continental Marxism. It was reformist in method and ethical in belief, allied with a heavy dose of trade-union pragmatism. It did not threaten traditional institutions (not even the monarchy), but wanted to use them for its improving purposes. Equally, British conservatism stood outside the tradition of continental reaction. A reactionary critic once remarked that the trouble with British conservatism was that it had not put the clock back by even one minute. It was a 'dispositional' conservatism that prided itself on its lack of fixed ideological positions, had learnt from Edmund Burke about the need to reform in order to preserve, from Disraeli about the need to attend to the condition of the whole nation, and espoused a statecraft designed to keep the ship of state afloat in choppy waters. Even British liberalism stood outside continental traditions, not least in its embrace (early in the 20th century) of a 'new' liberalism that acknowledged that liberty could often be enlarged rather than diminished by collective action.

This is why it can be misleading to describe the central tension of the British political tradition as that between collectivism and libertarianism. The dominant ideological forces in 20th-century British politics, on left and right, both believed in a strong state. The socialist left wanted to enlarge and deploy the state for its collectivist purposes, while the conservative right was attached to the state as the repository of authority and tradition. The left attacked the right for its selfish defence of privilege and inequality, and the right attacked the left for its divisive class envy and levelling ambitions. Yet behind these ferocious antagonisms, which were the stuff of much of 20th-century British politics, there were some important affinities between Tory democracy and socialist collectivism. As Samuel Beer pointed out in his classic study of *Modern British Politics* (1965), 'Socialist Democracy and Tory Democracy have a great deal in common', not least the fact that they shared an outlook that 'legitimizes a massive concentration of political power'.

These affinities helped to keep British democracy afloat in troubled times. With a left that was gradualist, reformist, and constitutional, and a right that was adaptive and responsive, there was much procedural common ground. Yet it was more than merely procedural. The left wanted to reform capitalism rather than abolish it, while the right was not imprisoned by the laissez-faire inheritance of 19th-century liberalism. It may have been pushing it a bit for the impish Harold Macmillan (later to become Conservative prime minister) to declare that conservatism was 'only a form of paternal socialism', but in the British context it does make a point. There were no ideological barriers to interference and intervention, on left or right. Both traditions believed in doing things to people (whether by desire or necessity) and in drawing upon the top–down inheritance of the British state for this purpose.

Yet this was the silent conversation, rooted in shared assumptions about political power. The noisy 20th-century conversation between left and right drowned it out. The left demanded social justice and equality, which the right denounced as a threat to liberty, which in turn the left described as a cloak for privilege. The left wanted planning, regulation, and ownership for the common good, while the right railed against the threat to enterprise and the perils of bureaucratic uniformity. The language of class confronted the categories of individualism. The right attacked the left for its divisive attachment to class over nation, the foreignness of its creed (routinely accompanied by references to the Soviet Union) and general lack of patriotism. The left attacked the right for wrapping itself in the flag, xenophobia, and Little Englanderism.

Someone listening in to the British political conversation at various points in the last hundred years would soon pick up these familiar cadences. What they would almost certainly miss, though, is the extent of the agreement about power and the political system. They would not hear powerful voices, on either left or right, arguing that the traditional concentration of power in Britain should be diffused and pluralized, with new centres of power and new accountabilities, or that citizenship should be reconstituted. This is nicely illustrated by a quick comparison of two post-1945 books on the political system, one from the Labour left (Harold Laski's *Reflections on the Constitution*, 1951) and one from the Tory right (Leo Amery's *Thoughts on the Constitution*, 1947). From their different ideological perspectives, both agreed that Britain's top-down, government-centred way of doing politics should be defended and protected. In Amery's Tory view, it was essentially an executive-led system, with a passive people, and it was only the liberals and radicals of the 19th century who had 'grievously misled' opinion on the fundamental historical truth that the British system was one of 'government of the people, for the people, with, but not by, the people'. Now turn to the socialist Laski, who saw the job of the people as 'the creation of a Government which can govern' and was opposed to anything (such as proportional representation or devolution) which threatened 'the stability of executive power'. Across the ideological boundary lines, here was a crucial affinity.

It was an affinity that lurked behind the noisy arguments of British politics, complicating any attempt to fit these arguments within the confines of a simple 'collectivism versus liberty' narrative. This becomes clear if we look briefly at the major doctrinal waves which have shaped the contours of British politics from the end of the Second World War to the recent past.

Three stand out. Let us personalize them by calling them the Attlee, Thatcher, and Blair revolutions. It does not matter that these individuals were not themselves innovative thinkers. What matters is that their periods of political leadership are associated with seismic shifts in the tectonic plates of British politics. They therefore provide the point of entry into indispensable arguments.

The Attlee revolution (Clement Attlee was prime minister in the 1945–51 Labour governments) inaugurated what is often called the 'post-war settlement', which endured in its essentials for a long generation. The landslide election of Labour's first majority government in 1945, with Churchill rejected as soon as the war was won, might have felt like a revolution at the time ('I am stunned and shocked by the country's treachery', declared the Conservative MP 'Chips' Channon to his diary), but it carried over into the post-war world the social solidarity of wartime with its ethos of 'fair shares for all'. There was a general determination not to return to the poverty, inequality, and unemployment of the pre-war years, and to use all the resources of the state to win the peace just as they had been so energetically mobilized to win the war. It was the high point of British social democratic collectivism, as industries were nationalized, redistribution advanced, and the welfare state constructed. It was also sternly centralizing, in the interests of equity and uniformity, and with an expanded state as the object and agency of change. As it was said at the time, it was a period when the gentlemen in Whitehall really did know best.

Even though the Attlee revolution had run out of steam by 1951, when the electorate opted again for Conservative 'freedom', it endured in its essentials for a further generation. There is room for argument about the exact extent of the doctrinal consensus between the 1950s and the 1970s, but not about its existence. The Attlee revolution was locked in. Labour constantly looked back to it with a nostalgic and reaffirming glow, uncertain about where the left should go next, disputing between its 'fundamentalists' and 'revisionists'. The Conservatives, in an explicit act of political adjustment, had accepted the framework of economic management (for full employment), a 'mixed' economy with a substantial public sector, and the commitment to social welfare bequeathed by the Attlee revolution. This was the 'Keynes-plus-Beveridge' world of post-war British politics.

It was the collapse of this world in the 1970s that provided the opening for the Thatcher revolution (Margaret Thatcher became leader of the Conservative Party in 1975 and was prime minister from 1979 to 1990). As the post-war settlement became unsettled, under the pressures of accelerating inflation, rising unemployment, and industrial strife (culminating in the notorious 'winter of discontent' of 1978–9), a 'new' right saw its opportunity to wage an intellectual and political assault on the whole set of assumptions that had underpinned post-war British politics, on both left and right. One of Mrs Thatcher's key intellectual lieutenants, Keith Joseph, captured the nature of the moment when he declared: 'It was only in April 1974 that I was converted to Conservatism. I had thought I was a Conservative, but I now see that I was not really one at all.' It was intended to be a revolutionary moment, and so it turned out.

In a decisive break from the accommodative traditions of 'one nation' conservatism, the Thatcherite apostles of the 'new', neo-liberal conservatism set about unpicking the post-war settlement. They attacked the bloated state and rolled back its frontiers in the name of market freedom (privatizing where the Attlee revolution had nationalized); championed self-reliance and denounced dependency; disciplined the trade unions in the cause of enterprise; and junked post-war ideas about social justice and equality in favour of a creed of individual mobility and liberty. Their model was the United States; their enemy was continental Europe. Their intellectual mentors included Friedrich von Hayek, the philosopher of the reduced state, and the philosopher of monetarist economics, Milton Friedman. It was Friedman who

5. Attlee and Thatcher: making and unmaking the post-war settlement

once described Mrs Thatcher as not being a Tory at all, but really 'a nineteenth-century liberal'.

This is a revealingly inaccurate phrase. If it captures the extent to which the new conservatism was different from the old, in its embrace of 19th-century free market liberalism, it completely misses the extent to which it was ferociously anti-liberal in its attachment to (and deployment of) the unchecked power of the centralized British state. Far from wanting to circumscribe this power, the Thatcher revolution sought energetically to exploit it to snuff out any alternative centres of power (such as local government, and the trade unions). It was not detained by the conventional rules of the constitutional game, and certainly did not want to construct any new ones that could inhibit what governments could do. Critical observers coined phrases such as 'authoritarian populism' and 'free market and strong state' to describe this aspect of the Thatcher revolution, at once liberal in economics and uncompromisingly Tory in politics.

It was a potent combination, which transformed the landscape of British politics. It certainly demolished the post-war settlement (Mrs Thatcher had famously described her purpose as the abolition of 'socialism' once and for all), but whether a new settlement had been established was less clear. This was the explicit purpose, and claim, of the Blair revolution that followed (Tony Blair became leader of the Labour Party in 1994 and prime minister from 1997 to 2007). One of his first acts as party leader had been to ditch the party's ancestral ideological statement with its commitment to public ownership. His New Labour credo was the need to reject the outlook of both the 'old left' (i.e. the Attlee revolution) and the 'new right' (i.e. the Thatcher revolution) in favour of a 'third way' synthesis that reconciled market economics with social justice, individualism with community, and rights with duties. It was impatient with traditional ideological categories, emphasized the need to adapt to a world in rapid and dynamic change ('a world that has taken us by surprise' in the words of Anthony Giddens, a leading thinker of the new dispensation), and insisted that 'what matters is what works'.

It was difficult to pin Blairism down. Its pick'n'mix kind of politics, with lions invited to lie down with lambs, confounded ancestral political arguments. There was much debate about what Blairism 'really' was. 'We are not crypto-Thatcherites. We are not old-style socialists. We are what we believe in. We are meritocrats. We believe in empowering all our people. We should celebrate not just those who are born well, but those who do well': this was Blair's own answer. It was an ideology for an age that seemed to have abandoned ideology. It stood for newism. Without coherent alternatives on left or right, it commanded the political landscape and carried all before it. The fact that nobody was quite sure what it was could seem like a positive advantage. Blair's 'big tent' was deliberately designed to cover as much political ground as possible. Internationally, Blair advanced a doctrine of 'liberal interventionism', but this came a cropper (as did Blair's own reputation) in the controversy and quagmire surrounding the Iraq invasion of 2003. Yet it was only when the political weather started to get rougher again, as it did with a vengeance once Gordon Brown had taken over from Tony Blair in 2007 and was soon engulfed by the banking crisis, that a new political environment demanded a new set of political responses.

So these were the three ideological tidal waves in post-1945 British politics, at least until very recently. Someone listening in to an imaginary conversation between Attlee, Thatcher, and Blair would soon pick up the dominant political themes of the past half-century. However, they would also hear something of the wider context of national debate and popular opinion behind these particular arguments. Much of this centred on a continuing and often anguished preoccupation with what was happening to Britain and what it now meant to be British. There was much talk of British 'decline' and how this could be remedied. Attachment to the old struggled with an embrace of the new. Politicians were constantly

6. New Labour's 'big tent' (Chris Riddell, *The Observer*, 3 October 1999)

invoking a 'new' Britain (both Margaret Thatcher and Tony Blair were self-styled modernizers), but this involved a reckoning with the considerable inheritance of 'old' Britain.

The key fronts in this struggle were class, race, and Europe, the salience of which varied at different periods. There was much lively argument for a long period about the extent to which Britain was class-ridden, stuffy, and in the grip of an old establishment (or, conversely, of the trade unions), and so needed a thorough shaking-up. The continuing political potency of class was still evident in 2012 as one Conservative MP attacked her own leaders as 'two posh boys who don't know the price of milk'; and a Conservative education minister could declare that 'those who were born poor are more likely to stay poor and those who inherit privilege are more likely to pass on privilege in England than in any comparable country'. Then there was the politics of race, which threatened to become incendiary at one point, as British society visibly changed under

47

the impact of large-scale immigration from the black Commonwealth. A Conservative politician provoked controversy by suggesting a 'cricket test' for ethnic minorities (did they support the English cricket team?); while a Labour politician (and foreign secretary) countered by describing Britain as having become a 'chicken tikka masala' society (as this was now its favourite dish). There is nothing more explosive than the politics of identity, and it has lurked just beneath the surface of British politics, testing to the limits a liberal tradition of tolerance and fuelling a politics of racism and anti-immigration that has established itself on the fringe of British politics and had an impact on the mainstream.

It also connects with the issue of Europe, which has been the running sore in British politics for much of the past half-century. It has divided parties and confounded normal ideological positions. Enthusiasts for European integration have warned of lost opportunities for Britain (often in metaphors about trains and boats being missed); while opponents have warned about the loss of identity and sovereignty (usually with gibes about rule by Brussels). It has been easier to excite public opinion about the threats than the opportunities. This has made even Euro-enthusiasts tread carefully.

> The tragedy for British politics – for Britain – has been that politicians of both parties have consistently failed, not just in the 1950s but on up to the present day, to appreciate the emerging reality of European integration.... The history of our engagement with Europe is one of opportunities missed in the name of illusions and Britain suffering as a result.

This was Tony Blair in November 2001. However a decade later, with the Eurozone in crisis, there was general political agreement that the decision not to join the European single currency had been an opportunity that it had been wise to miss. As even tighter integration emerged as the EU response to the crisis, new questions arose about where this left the position of Britain.

It also reignited the whole European issue in British politics, with Conservative MPs (under electoral challenge from the UK Independence Party) pressing their party leadership to use the crisis to wrest powers away from the EU and to hold a referendum on British membership. Having tried to subdue his party's obsession with Europe, Conservative leader David Cameron now felt its full force, promising to hold a future referendum.

His aim had been to become the 'heir to Blair'. Just as Blair had decontaminated the Labour brand, and made it electorally

LAST BUS

7. The last bus (or boat, or train) to Europe has been regularly sighted, as this Low cartoon from the 1950s shows (*Manchester Guardian*, 10 October 1956)

successful, so Cameron had set about decontaminating the Conservative brand. Where Blair had offered New Labour as his defining idea, Cameron offered a Big Society as his big idea which 'is about a huge culture change, where people, in their everyday lives, in their homes, in their neighbourhoods, in their workplace, don't always turn to officials, local authorities or central government for answers to the problems they face but instead feel both free and powerful enough to help themselves and their own communities'.

He wanted this to be the *leitmotif* of the Conservative/Liberal Democrat coalition government he headed in 2010: 'We need to turn government completely on its head. The rule of this government should be: if it unleashes community engagement we should do it; if it crushes it we shouldn't.' This gave a new ideological twist to a traditional Conservative anti-statism, but it was not clear what it might mean in practice. However, it was soon submerged by the impact of the financial crisis that dominated British politics from 2008 onwards and which then turned into prolonged economic recession. What defined the 2010 coalition government was not discussion about a big society but whether its austerity programme was working (and whether it was providing a cover for an old ideological ambition to reduce the size of the state). Moreover, the failure of regulation to prevent the financial crash had seemed to identify the need for more state, not less.

What the crash had produced was ideological disorientation on both left and right. The right's belief in free markets and light regulation had been undermined by the irresponsible behaviour of financial institutions and bankers. The left's attachment to a politics of public spending (sustained by tax receipts from Britain's large financial sector) had been undermined by the new politics of deficit reduction. Politicians in all parties lined up to proclaim their attachment to a more responsible version of capitalism. Labour's new leader, Ed Miliband, declared that the party's New

Labour period was over and launched an attack on a 'predatory' kind of capitalism that had to be converted into something more benign. All this was a recognition that something profound had happened, shattering previous assumptions; but it was far from clear where (or when) secure ideological ground of any kind would again be found, what its policy implications might be, and where the centre of political gravity would settle down. At the same time a range of new issues—many of them about identity, lifestyle, and culture—refused to be compressed into ancestral categories (and so did not feed a political culture war of the kind seen in the United States). One example of such issues was the row in early 2013 over gay marriage that divided the Conservatives. Thus, there was still plenty to argue about; but the arguments could no longer be contained within the old familiar boxes.

Chapter 4
Governing: the strong centre?

> I think a lot of things that I've done – a strong centre, making sure that the writ of the Prime Minister runs throughout – I think that's just an inevitable part of modern government. I don't apologise for it at all.
>
> (Tony Blair)

British government is strong government. This has been the big truth about British politics. It was evident in the response to the financial crisis in 2008. Having authorized a government guarantee of lending to the banks of £186 billion, Chancellor of the Exchequer Alistair Darling 'reflected that, unlike many of my international counterparts, I had the authority to do so, even if the Bank of England was reluctant, without having first to seek parliamentary authority'. Some people have celebrated this strength, because it gives direction and cohesion to the business of government. Others have lamented it, because it allows government to occupy too much political space. What we shall have to consider is whether recent constitutional and political changes, including the arrival of coalition government in 2010, mean that this traditional account of strong government needs to be revised. Before that, though, it is necessary to understand the basis for the traditional picture.

In discussing the constitution, we noticed how government had come to occupy the space it did. It was the product of a very particular history, in which the centrality of the governing function maintained a continuous existence despite all the other political developments going on around it. This is what Dicey meant when he wrote that 'the prerogatives of the Crown have become the privileges of the people', in the sense that the transition to democracy in Britain had been accomplished while retaining the governing authority historically enjoyed by the Crown: 'This curious process, by which the personal authority of the King has been turned into the sovereignty of the King in Parliament, has had two effects: it has put an end to the arbitrary powers of the monarch; and it has preserved intact and undiminished the supreme authority of the State'. This supreme authority was not pluralized or decisively constitutionalized. Nor was it merely preserved, though, for when government acquired a democratic basis this brought with it a new and powerful legitimacy for its supremacy in the shape of 'the people', represented by ever more organized parties.

It was certainly a 'curious' business. When Tony Blair was portrayed as 'the King in Parliament', even if it was not usually expressed in quite that way, this was the indispensable context. In a narrow sense, it reflected the fact that a range of prerogative powers that were formerly possessed by the monarch (for example, to make appointments, sign treaties, declare wars) had transferred intact to the prime minister, bypassing the legislature on the way. There were periodic suggestions that these prerogative powers needed to be constitutionalized in some way, but these were not suggestions that commended themselves to prime ministers or governments, at least until very recently. In a broader sense, the real curiosity of the business is the way in which the executive as a whole retained, and consolidated, its dominance within the political system. It was a top–down polity. This made Britain distinctive among democracies for its degree of concentrated and centralized power.

Leave aside for a moment the question of whether this portrait now requires serious revision, or whether its essential features remain intact. The prior task is to get the original portrait into proper focus. Several elements combined to define the whole. There was the executive's dominance of Parliament. There was an electoral system that eschewed proportionality in favour of the production of 'governments that can govern'. There was the absence of a codified constitution and of a constitutional court to protect it. There was the preference for conventions as the organizing principles of political life. There was the centre's control of the localities. There was a political culture organized around the clash of opposites, in the form of an actual government and a 'shadow' one, rather than a search for consensus, compromise, and coalition-building. There were the tight party disciplines that kept everything (and everybody) in shape.

This is why Britain has been described as the traditional exemplar of a 'power-hoarding' polity, in Anthony King's nice phrase. A strong executive centre had not wanted to share power with Parliament, other parties, judges, or local governments; and had resisted proposals (for example, to change the electoral system, or to strengthen the second chamber) that would check and circumscribe its governing authority. Behind this predisposition had been erected a legitimating narrative about the nature of government in Britain. Those in search of a classic summary need look no further than the Blair government's consultation document on House of Lords reform (*The House of Lords—Completing the Reform*, November 2001). In a short section of just six paragraphs, under the heading of 'The Pre-Eminence of the House of Commons', there is to be found a wonderfully distilled account of the official version of how Britain had come to be governed in the way that it had.

It deserves a wide readership. Unfortunately, only a brief précis is possible here. It goes like this. Britain has a 'tripartite sovereignty' of the Crown in both Houses of Parliament, but in practice the three parts have uneven powers. The Commons has become predominant and the Crown ('or Executive') has become accountable to Parliament. The electoral system 'enables the people to give a clear and unequivocal answer to the question "Whom do you choose to govern you?"', and the political system is 'built around that principle'. It produces a government formed by the majority party, and an official opposition from the largest rival party. Although the convention-based constitution is 'flexible enough to accommodate alternative arrangements', these occur only very exceptionally. This system has 'provided Britain with effective democratic Government and accountability for more than a century, and few would wish to change it'. It is founded on the 'pre-eminence of the House of Commons' and it is 'vital that reform of the Lords does not upset this balance'. The key requirement of any reform therefore is that it should not 'obscure the line of authority and accountability that flows between the people and those they elect directly to form the Government'.

Here is the traditional system described in all its governing simplicity. It is the job of the people to elect a government, and it is the job of the government to govern. Nothing should confuse, or get in the way of, the singular clarity of this political arrangement. Crown power had become executive power, and the legislative supremacy established by the House of Commons had secured the unfettered exercise of that power by a majority party. Note the absence in this account of any concern with checks and balances, or with the plurality and division of power, or with competing legitimacies: all the routine stuff of politics and political systems everywhere. So any argument that a reformed second chamber might be needed as part of an attempt to rebalance the political system, towards Parliament and against the executive, does not even merit consideration. The system's deliberately uneven balance was intrinsic to its single 'line of authority and accountability'. The fact that this line ended in the 'pre-eminence of the House of Commons', which was normally in the pocket of the executive, was not thought to raise questions about the easy conjoining of authority and accountability.

This was not always so. There was a time when good government was thought to require an explicit unbundling of power and accountability. As Peter Hennessy puts it: 'For a few brief years at the beginning of the eighteenth century it looked as if the country might consciously separate the powers of the executive and the legislature'. The 1701 Act of Settlement contained a provision that prohibited a monarchical placeman (a minister to us) from being a Member of Parliament. This provision was repealed (in 1705) before it could be implemented. Had it not been, British government would have developed quite differently. There would have been no easy elision of power from monarch to Cabinet and prime minister, and no fusion of executive and legislature as the operating principle of British government. Even into the 20th century there was a requirement that a Member of Parliament who was made a minister should stand for re-election, a residual attempt to separate out roles, but this too was abandoned once the

8. The Queen (Victoria) dissolving Parliament (*Punch*, 1847)

age of party government had established the ascendancy of the doctrine about a single line of authority and accountability.

So Britain became the home of 'strong government', with a vengeance. Formed from a single party (at least since 1945 and until the coalition of 2010), government controlled the House of Commons—more or less securely at different periods—and was able to convert the formal sovereignty of Parliament into the effective sovereignty of the executive. That executive is formally a collective one, in the shape of a Cabinet of ministers (supplemented by a larger cadre of subordinate ministers outside the Cabinet). Originally, in fact as well as in name, the King's ministers, they had eventually become ministers without the King as royal power was progressively stripped away. They became instead the ministers of the prime minister, who was formally commissioned to form a government by the monarch ('The Queen has invited me to form a government'), but in practice was the leader of the majority party who appointed ministers (and removed them) as he constructed 'his' government. Faced with the need, first, to present a united front against the monarch and, later, against Parliament and the electorate, a governing convention of 'collective cabinet responsibility' was developed to ensure a common line. As Lord Melbourne told his Cabinet in 1841 as they discussed the Corn Laws, 'we had better all tell the same story'. There have been moments of acute controversy when it has simply not been possible for ministers to tell the same story, requiring the convention to be temporarily suspended (for example, by Harold Wilson at the time of the Common Market referendum in 1975 and by the Conservative/Liberal Democrat coalition on the Alternative Vote referendum in 2011). In other circumstances, ministers who want to tell a different story are required to toe the line or resign.

Well, that's the theory. The practice is inevitably rather different. Even single-party governments contain different views, and interests, and opposition parties and the media spend much of their time trying to expose these (while ministers and their acolytes may also brief against each other). Coalition government puts additional strain on the convention and requires its generous interpretation. Much of the daily political debate in Britain, in the media and between the parties, seems to consist of attempts to show that government is not the united front it claims to be. Ditto for the 'shadow' government. This is a wearisome business for all concerned, and does little to advance intelligent political discussion. In fact, the effect is to close down free-range political argument. Sometimes it is patently obvious that a government is racked by internal divisions and differences. This was the fate of John Major's government in the 1990s on the issue of Europe (prompting Major to refer, in an unguarded moment, to the group of 'bastards' in his Cabinet). It was clear that they did not all tell the same story, let alone believe it; but it was also clear that the dissenters could not be removed or disciplined because they merely reflected equivalent divisions within the party. As for the Blair government, a running theme in all the commentary was the split between Tony Blair's Downing Street and Gordon Brown's Treasury, including on the issue of the single European currency. The language of 'split' (along with the language of 'U-turn') is never far from the British political debate.

Although we talk about 'the government', and the convention of collective responsibility that underpins this, this can be somewhat misleading as a description of how the business of governing Britain actually works. As a former head of the civil service, Sir William Armstrong, once put it: 'The first thing to be noted about the central government of this country is that it is a federation of departments'. Not all departments are equal though, and the Treasury is the most unequal of all. As the keeper of the purse, its tentacles extend everywhere. In the words of a former chancellor of the exchequer, Nigel Lawson, 'it is not for nothing that the Treasury is known in Whitehall as the Central Department'. This also makes the relationship between the prime minister and the chancellor by far the most crucial relationship within government.

When it breaks down (as happened between Mrs Thatcher and her chancellor, Nigel Lawson), a government is soon in trouble. This is why the troubled relationship between Tony Blair and Gordon Brown (now documented in gruesome detail in a range of memoirs) was so toxic for good government, reinforced by the fact that Gordon Brown's Treasury had invented a range of powerful new instruments with which to tighten its grip on the work of ministers and departments.

Yet it is through individual ministers that the business of government is formally conducted, and it is the ministerial head of each department (the secretary of state) who is charged with the formal responsibility for that department's activity (or inactivity). They have to account to Parliament—and to the prime minister, and to the media, and to the wider public—for what their department does. This is what the other governing

9. Tony Blair buries Cabinet government (Richard Willson, *The Times*, 5 January 1998)

Governing: the strong centre?

convention, that of 'individual ministerial responsibility', is all about. It is about carrying the can. Sometimes it may mean resignation when things go badly wrong, but ministers have been more likely to go when they have been found in occupancy of the wrong bed rather than in possession of a failed policy. There is perennial discussion about what the 'responsibility' and 'accountability' of ministers actually mean in practice, whether these terms are the same, and how such obligations are properly discharged. Those in search of enlightenment might consult the Ministerial Code, a sort of rule-book on conduct issued by the prime minister to all ministers in the government. This also contains the text of a resolution on ministerial responsibility passed by the House of Commons in 1997, in the wake of an inquiry into the Iraq arms sale scandal. For all its imprecision, the political accountability of ministers is fundamental to the conduct of British politics.

Ministers have all the resources of the civil service at their disposal. This is Britain's permanent government. Ministers (and governments) come and go, but civil servants stay. Apart from the small number of politically appointed special advisers that ministers are allowed (about whom there is periodic controversy), the politicians depend upon their civil servants for advancing their policy objectives. The deal is that ministers alone are politically responsible for their departments, each of which has a Permanent Secretary as its administrative head, with civil servants giving loyal service to their minister (of whatever party, bearing whatever policies) in exchange for anonymity and protection of their independence and impartiality. This produces a relationship of serial monogamy between civil servants and ministers (memorably satirized in the British television series *Yes, Minister*) that sits at the heart of government. Ministers want results, and quickly; civil servants want practicality, and proper process. This gives rise to inevitable, and necessary, tensions, including (from politicians) regular proposals for civil service reform.

There are further tensions between the departmental basis of government and the need for a collective strategy. The Cabinet is the formal mechanism to secure the latter (and can still go 'live' at certain moments, in certain governments), but in practice it increasingly rubber-stamps decisions rather than takes them. It has inherent limitations as a collective decision-making device, not least that identified by a former senior civil servant, Sir Douglas Wass, in 1983: 'No minister I know of has won political distinction by his performance in Cabinet or by his contribution to collective decision-making.' Much of the work of Cabinet is now processed through a system of Cabinet Committees, but many of the key decisions that are processed have already been taken in bilateral meetings between the prime minister (or those who act on his behalf) and individual ministers. In the Blair government Cabinet meetings were stripped down to their barest essentials, sometimes lasting for as little as 45 minutes, with the real business of government transacted elsewhere. A joke said to be circulating among ministers asked why only half the Cabinet drank tea: because Cabinet meetings were over before the trolley had gone all round the room. Blair started as he meant to go on. On the Sunday afternoon after the 1997 election, the momentous decision to transfer control over interest rates to the Bank of England was taken in a meeting between Gordon Brown and Tony Blair in the front room of Blair's family house in Islington. The journalist Andrew Rawnsley (in his *Servants of the People*) takes up the story of what happened the next day:

> The plan had brought Blair into another collision with the Cabinet Secretary about the centralist style of governing. Handing over control of monetary policy was, by any standards, a sensational step, and the more so because it had not been advertised in advance either to the electorate or anyone else in the Cabinet. When the Prime Minister allowed him into the secret, Sir Robin Butler was astounded to learn that Blair and Brown were planning to act without consulting any other ministers. The Cabinet would not meet until two days after the announcement. Butler suggested to Blair

that his senior colleagues should surely be involved in such a momentous change. The Prime Minister was not interested in giving the Cabinet a vote. 'I'm sure they'll agree,' responded Blair. The Cabinet Secretary persisted: shouldn't the Cabinet at least be informed? 'They'll all agree,' repeated Blair, more emphatically. Butler made a final attempt to convince Blair to follow what Britain's most senior civil servant regarded as the constitutional proprieties. 'How do you know that the Cabinet will agree with the decision when it's still a secret?' Blair replied very simply: 'They will.'

There is endless discussion about whether Cabinet government has now been replaced by prime ministerial government. Each period and each prime minister allows a new twist to be given to this debate. Thus Margaret Thatcher was 'strong', but was eventually brought down by her colleagues. John Major was 'weak', with the Cabinet stronger but with government more ineffective. Tony Blair was 'presidential', but this had more to do with a particular conjunction of circumstances—a huge majority, a willing party, a personal authority—than with a permanent alteration in Britain's governing arrangements. Once the circumstances change, as they can do dramatically, rapidly, and unexpectedly, then so does the centre of gravity within government. Blair's diminished popularity after the Iraq war eventually enabled Gordon Brown and his supporters to force his resignation. Gordon Brown began strong, but his dysfunctional style of governing soon made him very weak; while David Cameron has been required to negotiate the particular circumstances of coalition government. The truth is that a prime minister is both commanding and vulnerable. He dominates the political landscape, but this does not mean that he is in secure and permanent control of all that he surveys.

The conventional wisdom in Britain has been that coalition government is necessarily weak and unstable, lacking the cohesion, discipline, and governing authority that single-party government provides. The early experience of the Conservative/ Liberal Democrat coalition government formed in 2010 challenged this view (certainly if the comparison was with the Brown government that preceded it). Rooted in a formal coalition agreement, it combined functioning Cabinet government with an informal system for brokering disagreements. A study by the Constitution Unit concluded that in its first eighteen months the coalition 'set a model for harmonious and unified government which may prove hard to follow'. Tensions inevitably grew though, with continuing speculation about whether the coalition would hold together for the duration of the Parliament. It was a coalition government but not a coalition Parliament; and this was the source of its increasing difficulties.

A recurrent question is whether the British system of government by departments, linked by the formal machinery of Cabinet and its committees, lacks an effective centre to hold it all together and to drive it on. This is the case for a prime minister's department, which does not exist (part of a prime minister's vulnerability) but which Tony Blair had clearly sought to establish in everything but name both by his governing style and by his development of the Downing Street machine. As the authoritative political commentator Peter Riddell described this process: 'The far-reaching changes in 10 Downing Street and the Cabinet Office since the election have created a Prime Minister's department in all but name that resembles the Executive Office serving the President in Washington DC. But a typically British hybrid has been created: *West Wing* meets *Yes, Prime Minister*' (*The Times*, 25 June 2001). Blair was much criticized for subverting Cabinet government by an informal and centralizing style of 'sofa' government. However, when David Cameron came to office promising a different governing style it was not long before some of his government's problems were being attributed to a weakness at the Downing Street centre, which he then sought to strengthen.

Nothing so distinguished the Blair premiership (what Peter Hennessy calls a 'command premiership') as a restless quest for governing levers that worked when they were pulled. Too many of the existing ones turned out to be made of rubber, producing an ever more frantic search for new ones of more durable construction. A civil service that was distinguished by an elegance of governing process met a prime minister whose mantra was 'delivery' of the governing product. Britain's former top civil servant, Cabinet Secretary Sir Richard Wilson, confessed in evidence to the House of Commons Public Administration Select Committee in 2001 that this emphasis on delivery had come as a challenging novelty to the administrative machine: 'I do accept that what we are being asked to do now is different in kind from the things we have been asked to do in the past.' So there is a paradox here. A system of 'strong' government, the traditional hallmark of British politics, combined with a weakness of practical delivery mechanisms. Governing capacity, in a political sense, was not the same as policy effectiveness.

This directs attention away from the narrow terrain of the political centre to the wider world of 'governance' in Britain. This is the world of executive agencies, quangos, partnerships, regulators, contracted-out services, and all the rest of the dense and complex network of arrangements through which government now operates. The central executive, even when it can negotiate its own fissiparous tendencies, depends upon this vast and unwieldy apparatus for converting its policy ambitions into administrative results. It is scarcely surprising that a pull on the central levers can often seem to produce only a muffled and uncertain response. The Blair government (and Gordon Brown's Treasury in particular) initially seemed to believe that they could micro-manage everything from the centre, setting targets, controlling funds, and imposing disciplines. This is what 'strong government' permits. However, they soon discovered that this was far more difficult in practice than they had allowed for; and the emphasis began to switch to developing 'strategic capacity' at more local levels, with 'earned autonomy' for organizations which could demonstrate good management and delivery.

The 2010 coalition government led by David Cameron promised a radically different approach to governing, involving a rejection of statism and centralism. 'We want to turn government on its head', declared Cameron, 'taking power away from Whitehall and putting it in the hands of people and communities.' The coalition agreement promised 'radical devolution of power and greater financial autonomy to local government and community groups'. Instead of 'bureaucratic accountability' there would be 'democratic accountability'. Previously the emphasis had been on deploying all the resources of a strong centre to force improvement in how the state delivered its services; now the emphasis was on getting the state out of the picture and enabling others to take on the job.

So Whitehall numbers were culled, business outsiders brought in to oversee departments, and policy advice was to be contracted out. In the name of localism, local government was given more flexible powers and community groups more powers in relation to local government. In the name of accountability, all items of public spending would have to be logged and published. There would be elected police commissioners and public services like schools and hospitals increasingly freed from state control. A bonfire of quangos saw a range of public bodies either abolished or merged. Here was the centre wanting to offload responsibilities, but it was not clear whether it would represent a lasting transformation in how Britain was governed. Its critics alleged that it was really just about reducing the size and role of the state.

Part of the intention was to disperse power so that the central state would no longer be looked to for solutions to every problem. Yet this ran up against a political culture in which equity was preferred to diversity and the state was expected to provide a uniform level of service to its citizens wherever they lived. This suggested that the rhetoric of localism might be easier than its practice; while projections indicated that demands on the state, especially from an ageing population, were set to increase sharply in the future. There was also the enduring force of the political tradition of ministerial responsibility, which demanded accountability from government even if provision had gone elsewhere. In this sense a strong centre was rooted not just in control of the levers of government but in an established culture of expectations. Changing the latter was likely to prove more difficult than releasing the grip of the former.

If the centre is especially strong in Britain, it is at least in part because other centres of power are especially weak. Local democracy has virtually disappeared as the centre has tightened the screw. Although local government had never enjoyed any formal constitutional status, unlike the position of subnational governments in much of Europe, it had traditionally been protected by a custom and practice of separate spheres in Britain's informal constitutional arrangements. This changed sharply in the last two decades of the 20th century, when the centre snuffed out the vestigial independence of local government (the crucial constitutional moment was the 'capping' of local spending and taxing by the Thatcher government in the 1980s) and trampled all over the old conventions. Some 75 per cent of local authority spending now comes from the centre, which erodes the basis for a vibrant local democracy. The 'localism' of the Cameron government has not extended to restoring the taxing and spending power of local government. Similarly, although Scotland, Wales, and Northern Ireland now have forms of devolved government, England has not developed democratic regional institutions of its own. In this sense all roads still lead to the centre.

The British system of strong government also has some evident weaknesses. The strength comes from a political system in which the executive is in routine control of Parliament, and where institutional checks and balances of a formal kind have been largely absent. In this sense government in Britain is exceptionally, even uniquely, strong. It commands a wide political territory, has a large freedom of manœuvre, and possesses a formidable ability to translate policy ambitions into legislative achievements. This makes a British prime minister much less hemmed in, and constrained, than many of the other political leaders he encounters on his travels. Strong government gives a capacity for action, both at home and abroad, that represents a substantial asset. This being so, it may seem perverse to talk of associated weaknesses.

Yet these exist. Capacity for action is not the same as policy effectiveness. Post-1945 British history is distinguished by a running lamentation about the failure to halt decline, deal with entrenched problems, or keep up with other countries. This led some to suggest that the British system of alternating 'strong' governments produced policy lurches, prevented policy continuities, and failed to build durable consensus in key areas. Countries with much 'weaker' governments seemed, perversely, to have done rather better. So too with the centralization of the British system, which enabled government to ensure that its writ ran everywhere without check or hindrance, but also meant that there was a paucity of other institutions with the capacity for effective action. An ever more frantic pressing of buttons at the centre was a reflection of the weaknesses associated with such a lop-sided governing strength. An ever more complex network of control chains and coordinating mechanisms was required to keep the governing show on the road.

Then there were the changes from other directions, which posed huge challenges to the traditional British way of governing and required new governing techniques to be learnt. Engagement with the institutions of the European Union, which has formed an ever-increasing part of the lives of both ministers and civil servants, has introduced a pluralistic world of bargaining, negotiation, compromise, and coalition-building which stands in stark contrast to the winner-takes-all model of executive dominance which has distinguished the domestic political terrain (although the arrival of coalition government has required different governing techniques here too). As former prime minister John Major described the contrast in political styles: 'When British ministers spoke the language of Westminster in Brussels it was like spitting in church.' A tradition which boasted a 'sovereignty' that insisted on a single and inviolable source of governing authority met a tradition in which power was for sharing if this advanced the capacity for collective action. Similarly, while the rest of Europe saw 'federalism' in terms of dividing power, in Britain (where it was scarcely mentionable in polite society) it was understood as the centralization of power.

Other changes came from nearer home, many of them in the raft of constitutional reforms introduced by the Blair government after 1997. Their combined effect was to impose new checks on government and more pluralism in governing. Handing control of interest rates to the Bank of England imposed a major economic check. The Human Rights Act 1998 introduced a fundamental judicial check, involving a new discipline for the whole of government and bringing the courts into the business of government far beyond the judicial review of administrative action that had already grown in size and scope in the preceding years. The Freedom of Information Act 2000 brought a stronger informational check, involving a formal break with a traditional culture of secrecy and a wider window on the activities of government. Further checks came from new rules on party funding, and from new regulatory bodies like the Electoral Commission and official watchdogs such as the Committee on Standards in Public Life and (since 2010) The Office for Budget Responsibility. New conventions, such as the use of referendums for major constitutional changes, also became established. At the same time Parliament was becoming more assertive, chipping away at prerogative powers on matters such as war-making, treaty-making, and public appointments. All this meant that ministers and governments 'can no longer do what they were accustomed to do' (Bogdanor). Then there was the pluralizing of government, the conversion of a unitary state into a union state, that came with the creation of new forms of government in Scotland, Wales, and Northern Ireland (and with electoral systems that pluralized power in the same way that the Westminster system concentrated it). There was no longer a single British political system, but several political systems within Britain, while externally whole tracts of policy were now controlled or circumscribed by the European Union. Governing involved negotiating this new reality.

So the old portrait clearly does need some revision. Britain's political system is still, in comparative terms, a power-hoarding one, with supports for a strong centre remaining in place. Yet the supports are weaker and the governing constraints stronger. The arrival of coalition government in 2010 imposed further constraints in the form of political power-sharing, but in a sense this only reflected the power-sharing that had already taken place on other fronts. The real threat to strong government, as the financial crisis provided a brutal reminder, was from sources of power that individual national governments seemed unable or unwilling to control. Global financial power was unchecked by global financial governance. This was the challenge for governments everywhere and, in this respect at least, Britain was no exception.

Chapter 5

Representing: is the party over?

> Parties eat good men and spit them out bad…No nation's public
> life is so polluted by party as Britain's.
>
> (Simon Jenkins, *The Times*, 14 October 1998)

If you want to win votes and get elected in Britain, at least in
general elections, then you had better get a party. The occasional
and isolated exceptions only prove the rule. Before the 2010
general election, in the wake of the parliamentary expenses
scandal, there was speculation that independent candidates might
do unusually well, but in the event this did not happen. Elected
politicians have a wonderful capacity for persuading themselves
that their electoral success is to be explained by their obvious
personal qualities, but the evidence is all against them.
Overwhelmingly, it is the party label that counts. British politics is
party politics. This is another of the big truths. Yet parties
themselves are becoming weaker and the traditional party system
is less secure. This is something to which it will be necessary to
return.

Following the 1997 election, legislation was introduced
(Registration of Political Parties Act 1998) to enable parties to
register their title to their name, and to similar names that might
confuse the voters. The significance of this legislation was not
what it contained, which was relatively minor, but the fact that

legislation on political parties had been introduced at all. This was a major constitutional departure. The role of political parties might be one of the big truths of British politics, but it was a truth that had hitherto not dared to speak its name. Apart from some small housekeeping provisions, the existence of political parties was a closely guarded constitutional secret. This was like describing a car without mentioning that it had an engine.

It was not until 1969 that party names were even allowed to appear on ballot papers, finally exploding the fiction that it was individuals rather than parties who were being voted for. In the House of Commons the fiction is still maintained by the absence of any party designation in the way that MPs are formally described. They are simply the 'Honourable Member' for a particular constituency. The real business is done through a mysterious device known as the 'usual channels', curiously absent from the textbooks, where the party managers carve things up between themselves away from the decorous party-blind formalities of the chamber. But party has now come in from the constitutional cold. The legislation on party registration has been followed by a raft of other measures—on party list electoral arrangements for devolved assemblies and for the European Parliament, and regulation of party funding backed by a new commission—that bring the parties and the party system into full view.

So the secret is out. In Britain party rules. There might be argument about the extent to which the state should interfere with how voluntary associations like parties order their internal affairs, but not with the centrality of party to the operation of the political system. Tony Blair became prime minister because in 1983, just three weeks before the general election, a few members of the Trimdon branch of the safe Labour constituency of Sedgefield persuaded the 83-strong general committee of the local party, by the wafer-thin margin of 42 to 41, to add the young barrister's name to the shortlist from which it was selecting a parliamentary candidate. This is a vivid illustration of the way in which the parties act as the gatekeepers and recruiting agents of British political life. With no separation of powers, governments are formed from among the tiny pool of politicians who belong to the majority party in the House of Commons. Even coalition government only extends the pool slightly. These politicians are there not primarily because of the electorate but because of a prior election held by a small party 'selectorate', whose choice is then legitimized by the wider electorate.

In other words, the parties control the political process. While this is a feature of political life almost everywhere, in Britain the control exercised by the parties is exceptionally tight. Ever since Jonathan Swift satirized a Lilliputian world divided between High-Heelers and Low-Heelers (the issue at stake being the size of heels on shoes) and Big-Enders and Little-Enders (where the dispute is over which end of an egg should be broken first), the party question has been endlessly debated. Some saw party in terms of the evils of faction and sectionalism; others as (in Edmund Burke's words) 'a body of men united, for promoting by their joint endeavours the national interest, upon some particular principles in which they are all agreed'. The movement from loose associations of interests and persons to tightly organized electoral and parliamentary machines is the story of the development of the modern party system. It was a development that transformed political life. In the 1840s Sir James Graham, Peel's Home Secretary, described 'the state of Parties and of relative numbers' as 'the cardinal point', for 'with a majority in the House of Commons, everything is possible; without it, nothing can be done'.

The crucial period of transition was the 19th century. Some have looked back nostalgically to a mid-century 'golden age' before the grip of party had tightened, when governments could be made and unmade by shifting coalitions of parliamentary support; but the reality was rather different. In his *The English Constitution* (1867) Bagehot described the 'impotence' of political life without organized parties: 'It is not that you will not be able to do any good, but you will not be able to do anything at all. If everybody does what he thinks right, there will be 657 amendments to every motion, and none of them will be carried or the motion either'. This is a text that could hang above the desks of chief whips everywhere. It was after the 1867 Reform Act that party organization really took off, in response to the challenge of an enlarged urban electorate. Mass democracy produced mass parties (a process described by Ostrogorski in his *Democracy and the Organisation of Political Parties* (1902) as the 'methodical organisation of the electoral masses'). This aroused hope in some, and fear in others.

Parties are the organizers of political choice. This is a crucial function in any political system. In Britain the modern range of choice was shaped in the decade following the end of the First World War in 1918, with the final arrival of universal suffrage, the disappearance of troublesome Irish representation after the creation of the new Irish state, and the emergence of the infant Labour Party in place of the Liberals as the main alternative to the Conservatives. We became so accustomed to the post-1945 world of strong single-party governments and a two-party political system that it was easy to forget that an earlier world was quite different. Coalitions and minority governments were normal and the disciplines of party weaker (strikingly evidenced in the political career of Winston Churchill, who first left the Conservatives for the Liberals, then later moved back again). As the Jenkins Commission (set up by Tony Blair to look at the electoral system, as part of his deal with Liberal Democrat leader, Paddy Ashdown) put it in its 1998 report: 'On the factual record it clearly cannot be sustained that...there is anything shockingly unfamiliar to the British tradition about government depending upon a broader basis than single party whipped votes in the House of Commons'.

So the 'British model' was of more recent vintage than often supposed. At the beginning of the 1920s Britain had a three-party system; by the end of the 1920s it had effectively become a two-party system. At the general election of 1923 the Conservatives won 248 seats, Labour 191, and the Liberals 157; at the 1929 general election the equivalent figures were 249, 287, and 59 (and it was downhill all the way for the Liberals for decades after that). It was after 1945 that the British model of a 'classical' two-party system, the bedrock of 'strong' government, came into its own. The duopoly of two parties was established. From 1945 until 2010 Britain was governed either by the Labour or Conservative parties. At times majorities were fragile or even non-existent, but single-party government was sustained.

It was in the generation after 1945 that Britain came closest to the pure model of two party politics. During this period over 90 per cent of all votes went to the two main parties (peaking at 97 per cent in 1951). Class, ideology, and party seemed to have established a tight fit. In fact it was never quite as tight as it seemed (there was the much-examined 'anomaly' of the third of working-class people who voted Conservative, and evidence of disconnection on some issues between voters and 'their' parties), but it was probably as close as it could reasonably get. A textbook writer in the 1960s could confidently assert that 'class is the basis of British party politics; all else is embellishment and detail' (Pulzer). Then, after 1970, it all began to fall apart. On the surface it might seem the same, with governments still formed from one or other of the two big parties, but underneath there was radical discontinuity. Party competition went on as before, but the relationship between the parties and the electorate had undergone a profound change.

This is most strikingly seen in the sharply diminished share of the vote taken by the two main parties. Still at 89 per cent in 1970, this figure dropped to 75 per cent in 1974 and has never recovered since (and was 65 per cent in 2010). Labour's nadir came in 1983,

10. 'Find me a baby to kiss': Labour candidates canvassing, Cardiff, 1945

with only 28 per cent of the vote; while the Conservative nadir came in 1997 with 31 per cent. Another way of telling this story is to record the fact that from the 1970s elections were being won on a share of the vote that would have lost elections in the generation after 1945. The Conservative 'landslide' victory of 1983 was built on a vote share less than its share in the 1964 election when it lost; and Labour's landslide wins of 1997 and 2001 saw its share of the vote lower than when it lost in 1959.

The reasons are not hard to find. Other parties were more in evidence and took more votes. Between 1945 and 1966 in half the seats only Labour and the Conservatives put up candidates, but from 1974 all seats were contested by at least three parties. The Liberals received a boost with the SDP split from Labour in the early 1980s, while the nationalist parties in Scotland and Wales strengthened their position. More recently parties of the right (the BNP and UKIP) and of the left (the Greens and Respect) have added to the mix. Of these minority parties, the anti-EU UKIP has attracted most support, winning nearly 17 per cent of the vote at the 2009 European parliament election, but—unlike the Greens and Respect—not able to win even a single Westminster seat. Add in the evidence about a loosening link between class and party ('class dealignment' in the jargon, with 63 per cent of people voting for their 'natural' class party in the 1964 election but only 41 per cent in the 2005 election) and a marked weakening of the attachment felt by voters towards parties (a 'partisan dealignment' which saw 45 per cent of voters identifying very strongly with a political party in the 1960s but only 11 per cent doing so in the 2000s), and the cumulative picture becomes clear.

Yet for a long time it was concealed from view by a first-past-the-post electoral system that preserved the two-party dominance of the House of Commons. British politics therefore looked the same, even though it was not. In 1983 the combined vote share for Labour and the Conservatives fell to 70 per cent, but this still delivered them 93 per cent of the seats (and the Liberal Democrats, only a whisker behind Labour in votes, won a mere 23 seats to Labour's 209). The electoral system saved the two-party system. As long as the main parties retained their core support even when they were on the ropes, it was difficult for a third party whose support was evenly distributed to break through. The mismatch between a declining two-party system among the electorate and its survival at Westminster could be viewed in different ways. On one view what was being propped up was an obsolete adversarialism that failed to reflect the changed disposition of the electorate. However, on another view, it served to protect the stability of the political system against fragmenting tendencies that would render effective government more difficult.

There was a symmetry between a traditional winner-takes-all system of government, in which a governing majority in the House of Commons enjoyed largely unchecked power, and a winner-takes-all electoral system that usually delivered victory to a single party (despite the fact that no winning party since 1935 had secured over 50 per cent of the votes). Put together, here is what 'strong government' in Britain has meant. It has given unshared power to a party, and then given all the governing resources of a weakly constitutionalized polity to that party. This is winner-takes-all twice over. When a party government had a crushing majority in the House of Commons (as the Conservatives had in the 1980s, and Labour after 1997, prompting speculation in both cases about whether two-party politics had now become one-party politics), then it was even three times over.

The 2010 election, which failed to give a governing majority to any party, was the moment when the post-1945 party system finally succumbed to the erosion of its electoral foundations. In this sense the arrival of coalition government was not so much an aberration as a culmination. Not only did it bring Britain in line with the European norm, but brought Westminster in line with what was happening in the rest of the United Kingdom. It is no longer possible to describe something called 'the party system' in Britain, as there is now a variety of party systems. In Scotland and Wales (and with even more intricate power-sharing arrangements in Northern Ireland) there are new kinds of electoral systems

11. Winner takes all (*The Guardian*, 26 May 1990)

producing new kinds of governing systems. They are multi-party systems; and coalition politics has become routine (as it has in tracts of local government). All that had traditionally been seen as alien by the party system at Westminster, and as the unfortunate political habits of foreigners, had become the normal way of doing politics, now including Westminster too.

Yet the coalition agreement between Conservatives and Liberal Democrats had produced a government that nobody had voted for. What this meant was brought into sharp relief when the Liberal Democrats supported a policy on student fees that they had expressly repudiated during the election. Coalition government subverted the established conventions of political life, which were wonderfully simple and straightforward. They found their legitimating ideology in the doctrine of the mandate and the manifesto. A party told the electorate in its election manifesto (once a short and broad statement, now a long and detailed prospectus) what it would do if elected; and then claimed to have a mandate from the electorate for its actions in government.

The claim is spurious of course, at least in any precise sense, but that does not make it less potent. Manifestos are package deals, making it impossible to know which individual items are supported or disliked. The mandate rolls everything up together without discrimination. This enables politicians to claim that they 'have a mandate' for a particular policy when they may well have nothing of the kind, on the basis that the policy in question was 'in the manifesto'. This can be a way of deflecting criticism or stifling dissent. How could anyone possibly oppose something that the people had given a mandate for?

It was in this spirit that a junior minister wrote to the *Guardian* (5 January 2002) to take issue with an editorial that had criticized the government's plan to end jury trials for a range of cases. 'Given the importance you rightly attach to the voice of the people', declared the minister, 'I am surprised you ignore the manifesto on which this government was elected last June.... The people considered that manifesto and voted for it. You... may disagree with the proposal, but that is what the people voted for'. Here is the doctrine of manifesto and mandate deployed in its most brazen form. It is also absurd. Leave aside the fact that 'the people' in this case was represented by an electorate of whom only 59 per cent voted and only 23 per cent of those voted for the government. This attenuated people plainly did not 'consider' a proposal that made no appearance at all in the election campaign; and which was anyway not described in the small print of the manifesto as a curb on the right to trial by jury but as a craftily drafted promise to 'remove the widely abused right of defendants alone to dictate whether or not they should be tried in a crown court'. The attempt to mobilize the whole legitimating weight of the mandate doctrine in such a case was preposterous, serving only to expose its threadbare credentials, but it also provides a telling illustration of its central place in the armoury of party government. If coalition government is to become more usual, then there will be an expectation before an election (rather than, as in 2010, afterwards) that parties will indicate the terms upon which a coalition would be entered into.

Coalition also complicated the way in which parties had been able to exploit the resources of the British tradition of strong government. The arrival of democratic politics, and along with it the modern party system, bestowed a new legitimacy on this tradition by providing a direct transmission belt from the people's will to party government. Parliamentary sovereignty could now be identified with popular sovereignty, and the practical expression of both was the sovereignty of party (although there was a coyness about describing it in these terms). If party was the carrier of the people's will, then it was clearly right that it should hold unmediated sway. After all, who could gainsay the mandate bestowed by a sovereign people? The problem for a coalition government was that it did not have this kind of mandate, as it was a post-election arrangement made by the politicians.

It therefore had to advance an argument of necessity to justify its existence.

Party domination has inserted itself into every nook and cranny of British political life. The parties control the process of political recruitment, nationally and locally, and by extension also control (although now with some checks) the vast world of appointed government that sits alongside the narrower world of elected government. It is the patronage of party leaders that puts people into the House of Lords. The right of local parties to choose parliamentary candidates (in all parties) is jealously defended. The national party machines would much prefer to draft their own favoured people in if they could get away with it, and try various means to do so from time to time, but the local party selectorate remains firmly in charge of this gateway to political careers (and, on occasion, the exit route). There have been isolated experiments with primary elections involving the wider electorate, and proposals for a recall procedure in certain limited circumstances, but nothing that significantly alters the picture of party control.

All this raises issues about whom the local party selectorate is and how it operates. The rise of the Labour Party in the early years of the 20th century was in part a response to the refusal of local Liberal associations to select working-class candidates. Later in the century the making of 'new' Labour included a move to 'one member one vote' in candidate selection to break the hold of constituency activists who were regarded as unrepresentative of the party's members and voters. The embarrassing paucity of women being selected by all the parties prompted Labour to introduce women-only selections in some constituencies for the 1997 general election, producing a doubling in the number of women MPs at that election. Before 1987 women had never made up more than 5 per cent of MPs; after the 2010 election 22 per cent of MPs were women, the highest figure ever and the eleventh highest proportion of women MPs in the 27 EU member states.

The move to party-list elections would make it easier for representational imbalances to be tackled, but at the cost of greater central control of the political recruitment process.

It is not just entry to political life that the parties control, crucial though that is. Their control extends across the whole conduct of politics. They structure the policy choices that are presented to the voters. They produce the political leaders who form governments and oppositions. They organize the election campaigns. The whole of political argument in Britain is dominated by a permanent election campaign between the parties. Because each party aspires to form a government, in an electoral system that gives priority to government-forming over opinion-representing, they have to make a broad electoral appeal. If they seem to turn in upon themselves, becoming narrowly sectarian and rancorously divided (Labour in the 1980s, the Conservatives in the 1990s), electoral retribution is assured. The coalitions that were absent from the formal face of British politics between 1945 and 2010 were ever present in the internal life of the catch-all parties, which span an extraordinary range of opinion and interest. The arguments and deals that are the public face of politics in multi-party systems (and after 2010 in Britain) have in the past been transferred to the private life of the parties themselves. Coalition government has added inter-party to intra-party dissent.

This is reflected in the perennial issue of party management. This has historically been most acute in the Labour Party, for the party was the product of an extra-parliamentary movement that was organized on the basis of internal democracy. This brought endemic and inevitable tensions between the parliamentary leadership and the wider party. Some observers (as well as political opponents) even questioned whether Labour could function as a 'normal' parliamentary party. By contrast, the Conservatives were a resolutely 'top-down' party in which leaders were supposed to lead and followers to follow. The sharply different character of the annual conferences of the two parties used to serve as a vivid reminder of their respective internal cultures and structures. Now all this has changed. The parties operate in very similar ways. Although members may be asked to approve major policy documents, and are entitled to vote for party leaders, control and direction is firmly centralized in both the Labour and Conservative parties (rather less so in the case of the Liberal Democrats). Party management remains a permanent task, with plenty of opportunities for embarrassment and discomfort, but the traditional contrast between the two main parties on this front has largely disappeared. Indeed, dissent seems now to have become the hallmark of the Conservatives, posing the greatest threat to the Conservative-led coalition with the Liberal Democrats. It may also be that, in changed political circumstances, the ties that bind politicians to parties have started to become weaker.

Another issue has been how the parties are funded. The traditional position was that the Conservatives derived much of their money from business, and Labour from the trade unions. However by the 1990s both parties were increasingly dependent on income from wealthy individual donors. This became a source of considerable political controversy, with donors unidentified and allegations of money buying influence and rewards. When Labour came to power in 1997 it referred the whole issue of party funding to the Committee on Standards in Public Life, then legislated to implement the resulting report. This introduced transparency into political donations, with an electoral commission to monitor and regulate party finances, but this did not prevent continuing political controversy around the issue, most dramatically in 2006 when the police launched an investigation into 'cash for peerages'. Some believed that the only real solution was to be found in a system of state funding of political parties; but this seemed unlikely to commend itself to an electorate that was disposed to give less rather than more support to the parties. Further reports on the issue have appeared, most recently at the end of 2011, but inter-party agreement has remained elusive.

Parties are indispensable to the political process, yet 'party politics' is a routine term of political disapprobation in Britain. It suggests a rigid and predictable style of politics, in which the disciplines of party loyalty stifle independent thought and action. As Sidney Lowe put it: 'No sentiment is likely to elicit more applause at a public meeting, than the sentiment that "this, Mr Chairman, is not a party question, and I do not propose to treat it from a party standpoint"' (*The Governance of England*, 1904). Edmund Burke's famous speech in 1774 to the electors of Bristol, in which he announced that he was their representative but not their delegate, was difficult to transpose into an age when representatives had largely become the delegates of party. If politics without party is a recipe for impotence and chaos, the total domination of politics by party carries its own dangers.

This becomes a more acute issue as party membership declines; and as attachment to party weakens. Only the fringe parties buck these trends. In the early 1950s, the Conservatives had more than 3 million members and Labour over one million; but in 2010 Labour had 194,000 members, the Conservatives 177,000 and the Liberal Democrats 65,000. Only 1 per cent of the electorate was a member of one of the main parties, compared with nearly 4 per cent in 1983 and one of the lowest rates of party membership in Europe. This makes it harder to claim that parties are the uniquely legitimate channel of political representation. It is now frequently observed that the Royal Society for the Protection of Birds has more members than all the political parties put together. At one level this simply reflects the fact that people prefer birds to politicians, which is clearly not an irrational preference, but it also points to a dichotomy between a society which is ever more diverse in its composition, tastes, beliefs, and interests and a political process in which the parties retain a tight grip on almost everything that moves.

Of course in practice there is a vast representational network through which society presses its extraordinary (and often conflicting) range of demands and interests upon the politicians, and the parties are required to broker all this into some kind of politically manageable and coherent form. That is an absolutely vital function. It is also why some of the attacks on party are badly misplaced. Yet in the British context it does make sense to ask if party now claims too much for itself, and in particular if it claims too much political and representational territory. The fact that 99 per cent of people in Britain do not belong to a political party raises questions about the role of party as the gatekeeper of all public life. The disciplines of catch-all parties can make them very blunt representational instruments. This suggests that there is a case for putting some public interest regulation around the activities of parties, and for ensuring that they do not claim a monopoly of representational space. It also suggests that parties themselves need to change the way they operate.

Something is already happening to the representative system. This system was designed to demarcate the space between governing and being governed. It was the job of the electorate to put governments in and to boot them out; but it was the job of the politicians to do the governing. Thus the conventional political wisdom in Britain was that the referendum was a dangerous foreign device that was incompatible with the British system of parliamentary representation. It was associated with dangerous populism and the techniques of tyranny. As Clement Attlee declared in 1945: 'I could not consent to the introduction into our national life of a device so alien to all our traditions as the referendum.' Yet now the modern conventional wisdom is that major constitutional changes should routinely be approved by referendum. This constitutional innovation may have originated as an expedient to contain internal party divisions over the European issue in the 1970s, but the expedient has now become the expectation. Perhaps this reflects a disenchantment with politicians and with Parliament, or a diminished belief by politicians in themselves. It might also be thought to reflect a new enthusiasm for political participation, but for the fact (seen in the referendum on the electoral system in 2010, and on elected mayors in 2012) that there seems to be a marked disinclination by people to take part in this form of direct democracy. Perhaps the issue of Europe may prove to be the exception, following David Cameron's promise in 2013 ('it is time to settle this European question in British politics') of an in/out referendum after the next election if the Conservatives won. An old model of representation may have been abandoned; but this does not mean that a new one has been embraced.

Chapter 6
Accounting: heckling the steamroller?

When in that House MPs divide,
If they've got a brain and cerebellum too,
They've got to leave that brain outside
And vote just as their leaders tell' em to.
(Gilbert and Sullivan, *Iolanthe*)

A few weeks after my election to the House of Commons in 1992, one of my children asked what was the best bit so far about being a Member of Parliament. I remember saying that I thought there were two best bits. First, the fact that the library research staff would instantly provide you with a brief on any subject under the sun. My son thought this would be very useful for his homework. Second, the supply of yellow forms on which questions could be written to any Cabinet minister requesting information on anything that came within the minister's area of responsibility, with an obligation for an answer containing the information to be given (and published in Hansard, the parliamentary record) within a matter of days.

My son was disbelieving at such an extraordinary facility. So we agreed that we would put it to the test. But what to ask about? After some thought we suggested an esoteric question about the dangers of milk floats, on the basis that when I was my son's age I had crashed into one on my bike early one morning while delivering newspapers and had long harboured a grudge against them. This was duly agreed, and the yellow form was filled in and submitted. A few days later the following reply was received, as recorded in the Hansard record (30 June 1992):

Milk Floats

Dr. Wright: To ask the Secretary of State for Transport what figures are available on the number of accidents and injuries associated with milk floats.

Mr. Kenneth Carlisle: Milk floats cannot be specifically identified from accident records held by the Department. However, using vehicle registration marks, additional vehicle information is obtained from the Driver and Vehicle Licensing Agency at Swansea for about 80 per cent of vehicles involved in injury accidents. The table shows information on injury accidents in 1990 where DVLA data indicate the involvement of floats. The 1991 data are not yet available.

Injury accidents involving floats and casualties in those accidents: by float propulsion type: Great Britain: 1990

Propulsion type	Injury accidents	Casualties		
		Fatal	Serious	Slight
Electric	124	3	31	126
Other	64	1	14	70

Pandora's box was henceforth to be forever open. The people's representatives had to be answered by the mighty. Accountability was not a stale word but a continuous practice. The episode had a further twist when a journalist phoned to ask what I thought about the answer I had received and about my general views on the dangers of milk floats. My reply, now that I was warming to the theme, duly appeared in his newspaper. I had become the authority on milk floats. More than that, I realized that I had become someone whose half-baked views on all sorts of topics would henceforth be taken with all the seriousness that they had never previously been thought to deserve. In fact, I was surrounded by people whose utterances were being taken seriously, especially by themselves, and solemnly recorded for posterity. Parliamentary democracy was clearly a wonderful thing.

Yet the reality is rather different. Once the ceremonial veneer is stripped away, and the rhetorical fog of parliamentary sovereignty is allowed to clear, the fragility of accountability in a system in which the government controls the legislature produces a more complicated picture. A weak parliament has been the other face of strong government. What this has meant in practice was once nicely described (by Austin Mitchell MP in his splendidly entertaining *Westminster Man*) as like 'heckling a steamroller'. The heckling is loud and raucous, but the executive steamroller takes it all in its stride and gets on with its governing business. It may not always be smooth, but the bumpy bits are a small price to pay for undisputed occupancy of the wheel. That, at least, is the traditional picture. We need to ask if the recent history of Parliament (and politics) has modified this picture in any significant way; and where Parliament now sits in the account-holding business.

Tony Blair told the assembled ranks of Labour MPs elected in the party's landslide victory of 1997 that their job was to be 'ambassadors' for the government in their constituencies. That this was no mere rhetorical flourish, or statement of the politically obvious, was reflected in the fact that the party made arrangements for MPs to be away from Westminster for a week at a time and to be removed from the select committees that scrutinized government so that they could engage in campaign roles for the party. What seemed shocking about an arrangement of this kind was its brutal recognition of political reality. Had

Mr Blair lectured his new recruits on their duties of scrutiny and accountability as Members of Parliament that would have been even more genuinely shocking. Yet these duties are an indispensable part of what Parliament is supposed to be for.

Governments need to be held to account for what they do (and on a continuous basis, not just on the periodic days of electoral reckoning). This happens in various ways, notably through the media, but it is Parliament that is constitutionally charged with this responsibility, on behalf of the people. The formal procedures and conventions of Parliament (although two Houses, Commons and Lords, it is usually made synonymous with the Commons) are reflections of this purpose and duty. Ministers are required to attend Parliament regularly to answer questions and make statements, both to the full House and to its committees, as well as providing information in writing. Misleading or misinforming Parliament is the gravest ministerial sin, for which the highest political penalty is demanded. Legislation can only be passed after it has undergone an elaborate process of parliamentary examination and approval. Governments can only survive if they command sufficient parliamentary support, as tested by a vote of confidence.

All this constitutes a formidable armoury of parliamentary accountability, reflecting the primacy of the constitutional doctrine of the sovereignty of Parliament. The problem is that it also provides a misleading picture of how Parliament actually works and what it really does. In fact it is somewhat misleading to refer to 'Parliament' at all, as though it had a collective identity. It is useful for ministers to be able to describe it in this collective way ('Parliament has approved this measure', etc.), because it confers legitimacy on executive actions, but it is inaccurate as a description of how Parliament is organized and operates. Parliament in a collective sense does not really exist, or only sporadically. What does exist is a place where government and opposition meet to do battle in the permanent election campaign that defines and dominates British politics.

This is why the daily question time to ministers, and once a week to the prime minister, takes the form it does. It is the daily opportunity for the rival parliamentary armies to lob custard pies at each other (although the most lethal ones come from stroppy footsoldiers on your own side). These can be daunting occasions for ministers, and for prime ministers. In his memoirs Tony Blair, a consummate performer, described Prime Minister's Questions as 'the most nerve-racking, discombobulating, nail-biting, bowel-moving, terror-inspiring, courage-draining experience in my prime ministerial life, without question'. Yet (as he also pointed out) it is not really very effective in terms of accountability.

Of course Parliament engages in a whole range of activities. It provides a forum for national debate. Every issue under the sun will be raised by somebody. It allows MPs to pursue the grievances of their constituents and to highlight the needs of their constituencies, with direct access to ministers. It grants money ('supply') to government, originally its key function but now a largely unexamined formality. It considers and approves legislation, using public bill committees. It scrutinizes the continuing work and policies of government, especially through the departmental select committee system that has developed since 1979. It provides a training and proving ground for potential ministers. And, most crucially, it supplies the support for government and opposition.

There is enough in all of this to keep Members of Parliament frenetically busy. Whether it is busyness for a purpose, or the busyness of a hamster on a wheel, is another matter. This is Gyles Brandreth's diary record of a parliamentary day during his spell as a Conservative MP in the early 1990s, one of those 'scurrying like dervishes round the bottom of the greasy pole':

We're here every day, from breakfast till midnight (the *average* time of finishing has been midnight this session), darting from one

committee to the next, signing letters, tabling questions, meeting
constituents, being busy, busy, busy – but, frankly, to how much
avail? Today I've done the Railways Bill, bench duty, a question to
the Secretary of State for Health, a question to the PM, a Ten
Minute Rule Bill...I've not stopped...But really, was there any
point to it at all?

Of course, what he really wanted to be was a minister (he only
became a junior whip). That was the real purpose behind
such displays of parliamentary energy. In this he is entirely
representative of most Members of Parliament. It is this
which lies at the heart of the issue of accountability in Britain.
Parliamentary footsoldiers dream of one day holding a
ministerial baton. Put differently, this means that the real
ambition of most members of the legislature is to join the
executive. It is only necessary to record this for it to be apparent
why there is an intrinsic problem about accountability in such a
system, apart from the routinized accountability that comes
from having an official opposition. This is why the textbook talk
about Parliament's role in scrutiny and accountability frequently
fails to get inside the skin of an institution many of whose
members have a quite different agenda.

Contrary to common belief, the power of the party whips is the
consequence, not cause, of such considerations. Except in rare
circumstances, members vote for the party line not because they
are coerced into doing so but because they want to. A particularly
toadyish question to a minister is often greeted with the cry of
'Give him a job!' If a Member of Parliament is said to have been
given a 'job', the job in question will not be a parliamentary job
(such as the chair of a select committee) but one in the executive
(or shadow executive). This contrasts sharply with countries
where the legislature is stronger. There has been no career
structure for a politician within Parliament itself, only through
joining the ranks of the executive, although this may now be
changing as a result of recent developments.

Just in terms of numbers, the executive's hold on Parliament is tight (and over the years has become even tighter). Cabinet ministers are supplemented by a raft of more junior ministers, while a further raft of unpaid parliamentary aides (known as parliamentary private secretaries or PPSs) supplement both. The effect of this is that somewhere between a third and a half of members of the governing party in the House of Commons are effectively on the permanent executive 'payroll' vote, and so subject to the disciplines of collective responsibility. This proportion has also been increasing. Executive control on this scale necessarily saps the independence of the legislature (although one of the effects of coalition government since 2010 has been to reduce the number of ministerial jobs available to Conservative MPs, which has helped to fuel their discontent). It is not just that there is a desire to join the executive on the part of most Members of Parliament, but that the executive can normally accommodate this desire to a significant degree. The proposal by the Conservative-led coalition to reduce the number of MPs, without at the same time reducing the number of ministers, would have the effect of tilting this balance even further towards the executive.

The daily life of the House of Commons reflects the dilemma of accountability in a political system with fused rather than separated powers between executive and legislature. The fact that the results of parliamentary votes are routinely known in advance gives a sterile quality to much debate. In fact 'debate' is really a misnomer for what are usually prepared speeches served up to a largely empty chamber in which neither minds nor votes are likely to be changed by what is said. This gives a ritual character to proceedings. Even the anger is often synthetic. Hanging about Westminster waiting for votes is one of the main parliamentary activities. It is only on those occasions when an issue divides parties, and makes the result of votes uncertain, that the chamber springs into life. In recent years there have been an increasing number of such occasions.

Members of Parliament are bombarded with representations from pressure groups and others about all the issues of the day, especially in the context of legislation and votes, as though they were dispassionate and independent legislators rather than whipped members of their parties (although some groups, more sensibly, have now learned to direct their main legislative attention to the House of Lords where the party grip is weaker). It would be nice to record that the 1935 diary entry of 'Chips' Channon, then a new Conservative MP, is an historical eccentricity: 'Most of the day at the House of Commons. Today for the first time I really liked it; boredom passed and a glow of pleasure filtered through me. But I wish I sometimes *understood* what I was voting for, and what against'. Alas, it is not. It is a running joke among MPs that they frequently do not have a clue what they are voting for (or against). The whips are always there to point them helpfully into the right lobby. On those infrequent occasions when there are 'free' (unwhipped) votes, it is not unusual for there to be scenes of confusion as Members try to work out which voting lobby they should be in.

The extent to which Parliament (and crucially the House of Commons) is an ineffective instrument of accountability is most apparent in its scrutiny of legislation. In outward form legislation is carefully scrutinized through an elaborate series of parliamentary stages, including detailed consideration in committee. The reality is that the whole process is firmly controlled by the government, serious scrutiny by government members is actively discouraged, any concession or amendment is viewed as a sign of weakness, and the opposition plays a game of delay. The result is that much legislation is defective, vast quantities of amendments have to be introduced by the government at the House of Lords stage, and the government's control of the parliamentary timetable means that many of these amendments are then simply voted through by the Commons without any scrutiny at all. It is all deeply unsatisfactory, and felt to be so by almost everyone involved in it.

MONDAY 16TH DECEMBER 2002

SECOND READING OF THE HUNTING BILL

THERE WILL BE A FREE VOTE

TUESDAY 17TH DECEMBER 2002

SECOND READING OF THE PLANNING AND COMPULSORY PURCHASE BILL.

THERE WILL BE A THREE LINE WHIP AT 9.00PM FOR 10.00PM.

WEDNESDAY 18TH DECEMBER 2002

CONSIDERATION IN COMMITTEE OF THE REGIONAL ASSEMBLIES (PREPARATIONS) BILL

THERE WILL BE A RUNNING THREE LINE WHIP FROM 3.30PM.

THURSDAY 19TH DECEMBER 2002

MOTION ON THE CHRISTMAS RECESS ADJOURNMENT.

THERE WILL BE A ONE LINE WHIP.

FRIDAY 20TH DECEMBER 2002

THE HOUSE WILL NOT BE SITTING.

12. Whipping them in: this is an example of the 'whip' that goes to MPs from the Chief Whip of their party every week when the Commons is in session

It is sometimes suggested that Parliament does much better on the accountability front when it comes to the system of select committees which monitor the general work of government, mainly mirroring departments, and which have developed in their modern form since 1979. There is some truth in this. These committees conduct inquiries and issue reports, and endeavour (unlike the rest of the Commons) to operate on a consensual and bipartisan basis. This bestows a certain amount of authority on their work. However, they have suffered from a number of important limitations. Their membership has been in the gift of the party managers; they have been woefully under-resourced

British Politics

(with the exception of the Public Accounts Committee, which is serviced by the National Audit Office); their ability to undertake financial scrutiny of departments has been poor; there has been no right for their reports to be debated, let alone voted on; their ability to undertake inquiries has been restricted by their inability to access all relevant papers; and the fact that they have not provided an alternative career route to joining the executive for energetic and able Members of Parliament has meant that political and personal commitment to them has been weak. We shall have to consider in a moment whether, as a result of recent changes, this picture now needs revision. Before that, though, an important caveat has to be entered about the description of Parliament offered so far. This is the extent to which the formal accountability deficit is offset by the informal accountability that operates within the parliamentary parties themselves. In simplest terms, a government needs continuously to ensure that it is carrying its parliamentary supporters with it both on the broad direction of the government and on specific policies. When its majority is small (the Major government of 1992–7) this imperative is obviously greater than when it is huge (the Blair government after 1997), but it is always a continuing requirement of government. Coalition government after 2010 meant that members of two parliamentary parties had to be kept on board. There is a constant process of representation and negotiation between ministers and their parliamentary supporters, especially on contentious issues. Deals are struck and amendments made. Sometimes a measure is withdrawn or a vote not held (as on House of Lords reform in 2012, when Conservative rebellion threatened to defeat it), which is why 'dissidence' in the division lobbies only captures the formal face—and failure—of a continuous process of political accountability.

However, this formal face is not what it once was. For much of the twentieth century it was commonplace to lament the 'decline' of Parliament, with MPs described as having become mere lobby-fodder. 'As things are now', wrote Hollis in his 1949 book *Can Parliament Survive?*, 'it would really be simpler and more economical to keep a flock of tame sheep and from time to time drive them through the division lobbies.' In the 1960s a seminal study of British politics by the American political scientist Samuel Beer observed that party cohesion at Westminster had become 'so close to 100 per cent that there was no longer any point in measuring it'. Yet this ceased to be true almost as soon as it was written. From the 1970s onwards dissidence began to grow and in recent years has accelerated. This reflected a weakening of the ferocious tribalism that had been sustained by sharp ideological division. The Blair government's decision to take military action against Iraq led, in March 2003, to the biggest party rebellion in the division lobbies in modern parliamentary history. A habit of dissidence has also been evident, especially among Conservative MPs, during the post-2010 coalition government, fuelled by antipathy to their coalition partners. All this does not mean that Parliament has become a different kind of institution; but it does mean that it no longer fits the supine stereotype that used to be applied to it.

It might have been supposed that this would have done something to raise Parliament's reputation with the public. Instead, the reputation of both the institution and its Members was battered to pieces by the parliamentary expenses scandal that exploded in 2009. Using the new freedom of information provisions, it was revealed that a large number of Members of Parliament had been exploiting the lax rules governing their expenses and allowances to put money into their own pockets. The media and public uproar that followed these revelations was tremendous and threatened parliamentary meltdown. As a Commons committee set up in the wake of the scandal declared: 'the House of Commons is going through a crisis of confidence not experienced in our lifetimes . . . It is not too much to say that the institution is in crisis' (*Rebuilding the House*, 2009).

The crisis brought a number of consequences. Many disgraced MPs left the Commons; a handful went to prison. This in turn brought an unusually large number of new MPs into the Commons at the 2010 general election. An independent regulator was established to set MPs' pay and allowances. Perhaps most significant of all, the crisis offered a window of opportunity to make changes to how the Commons worked, especially in relation to the executive, in the hope that a more vigorous institution would be able to demonstrate its relevance and so help to restore its reputation. That, at least, was the argument advanced by the Reform Committee (under my chairmanship) established by Gordon Brown in the dying days of the 2005–10 Parliament.

There had been a 'modernization' committee in the Commons during the Blair years, but although this had produced various procedural changes (including shorter days) these were more concerned with enabling business to be processed more efficiently than with equipping Parliament with the means for holding governments to account more effectively. This latter purpose was the focus of the Reform Committee's proposals. It argued that select committees should have their chairs and members no longer appointed by the party machines—the scrutinized choosing the scrutineers—but by election. This, it was suggested, would bring both a higher political profile and more legitimacy to these scrutiny committees. At the same time, it was argued that the Commons should have more ability to control its own business, which since the end of the nineteenth century had come to be controlled almost entirely by the government, so that it could debate and vote on matters of its own choosing. Along with proposals to strengthen the role of public petitions, this was a package of reforms that, in normal times, would almost certainly have been resisted by the party machines (as had been the fate of previous reform initiatives).

However, the expenses scandal had ensured that these were not normal times. Encouraged by a reforming Speaker, these proposals

97

were approved without serious opposition before the 2010 general election and implemented soon after it. Although it is still too early to make a final judgement about their effects, it is already clear that they are making a difference both to how the Commons works and how it is perceived. The select committees have a much higher profile, memorably seen in the public hearings on the phone-hacking scandal and in the interrogation of disgraced bankers. Fortified by election, select committee chairs are becoming public figures in their own right and MPs are discovering that the committees can provide them with a parliamentary career structure that does not involve joining the executive.

At the same time the new ability of the Commons to determine some of its own business has produced debates and votes on matters which the government (and opposition) might well have preferred to keep off the parliamentary agenda. From the voting rights of prisoners to the issue of a referendum on the EU (prompting a massive Conservative rebellion), the Commons has been enlivened by these backbench motions and their often uncertain outcomes. Public petitions have also fed into this process. From its nadir in 2009, when it seemed to be in terminal decline, the Commons had begun to look like a more interesting place.

In fact, from a number of directions, the accountability role of the Commons has been strengthened during the first decade or so of this century, in addition to the more independent spirit of many of its Members. Changes to the public bill committees that examine legislation, enabling evidence-taking, have brought the promise of better scrutiny and improved legislation. The select committees have sharpened up their act, if still in need of improved forensic skills, and have acquired a role in vetting key public appointments. Parliament has reined in prerogative power on war-making and treaty-making. Prime ministers now have to account regularly to a parliamentary committee. All this represents a shift in the terms of trade between Parliament and the executive that was long overdue, in which strong government begins to be matched by stronger accountability. It may be time to stop lamenting the decline of Parliament from some mythical golden age, usually located somewhere in the middle of the nineteenth century (a period more accurately described by Gladstone in the 1850s as 'the paralysis of Parliament'), and start celebrating its recent rise. The steamroller trundles on, but the heckling is better organized and makes for a bumpier ride.

Then there is the House of Lords. There is always the House of Lords. Ever since the Parliament Act 1911, which reduced the power of the Lords to that of delay, declared a future intention 'to substitute for the House of Lords as it at present exists a Second Chamber constituted on a popular instead of hereditary basis', the matter of House of Lords reform has been one of the hardy annuals of British politics. Since 1997 alone there has been a royal commission, committee reports, white papers, joint committees, draft legislation, bills, parliamentary debates, and votes. The result of all this activity has been the removal of most (but not all) of the hereditary peers and with them the entrenched Conservative majority in the Lords. What has not resulted is any agreement on how this semi-reformed Lords, now appointed largely by the patronage power of party leaders, might move through a promised 'second stage' of reform to its final shape.

A House of Lords reform measure was part of the Conservative coalition deal with the Liberal Democrats in 2010, promising a predominately elected second chamber, but when a bill was produced in 2012 giving effect to this it had to be abandoned in the face of concerted Conservative opposition. It was yet another episode in the long saga of failed Lords reform. Yet even in its semi-reformed state, the Lords has become more assertive (and successful) in getting the Commons to think again about aspects of legislation. In this sense the Lords has also added to the strengthening of accountability that has taken place in the Commons, so enhancing the accountability capacity of Parliament as a whole.

But accountable to whom? This raises the vexed question of legitimacy that is never far from debate about the Lords. Does legitimacy in a democracy necessarily entail election? Or does the primacy of the elected Commons mean that a second and subordinate chamber could be constituted on a different basis? These are not abstract or academic questions. When a Member of Parliament, I received an irate call one day from a party whip who had heard that I was intending to support an amendment to a bill that had been made in the Lords. 'These people are not elected you know,' was his argument. In other words, they were not legitimate and so should be disregarded. When I pointed out that he did not want them to be elected (and that I thought on the issue in question they were right), he put the phone down. He now sits in the Lords. So legitimacy matters. That is why so much of the debate on Lords reform has centred on the respective merits of election and appointment.

Yet this should not be the only argument. There is broad agreement that a deliberative second chamber, able to revise and review, adds to the armoury of accountability in Britain. It should be neither rival nor replica of the Commons, but a partner. Instead of seeing a more legitimate and confident Lords as a threat to the primacy of the Commons (which, in terms of powers, it could not be), it would be more sensible to see it as strengthening the scrutiny and accountability role of Parliament as a whole. However, none of this makes comprehensive reform of the Lords any easier politically, which is why reform has come (if at all) only incrementally. It would require a huge investment of political capital and energy on the part of a government to drive radical reform through in the face of entrenched resistance. This does not seem likely any time soon.

It may be thought that this focus on Parliament in relation to the business of holding power to account is rather old-fashioned. There is some truth in this. Accountability operates in a whole variety of ways and through many different channels. Simply to

13. 'There is always the House of Lords...' (Peter Brookes, *The Times*, 12 July 2012)

focus on Parliament as the formal arena of accountability is clearly inadequate. For example, the media play a key role. A grilling by John Humphrys on the *Today* programme or a mauling at the hands of Jeremy Paxman on *Newsnight* is a much more formidable (and visible) exercise in accountability for a politician than what happens in the House of Commons. Instead of the media feeding off Parliament, as was once the case, it is now more common for Parliament to feed off the media.

Then there is the whole army of regulators, auditors, inspectors, investigators, and watchdogs which now presides over every nook and cranny of the public realm (and those parts of the private sector, such as the privatized utility companies or financial services industry, which are deemed to have a public interest). There is a committee to keep an eye on standards in public life, a commission to protect the integrity of the civil service, and another to watch over elections. An information commissioner protects openness, an Ombudsman is on permanent patrol to hear complaints from dissatisfied citizens, while the judges have developed a much more activist role in reviewing what governments do.

It is only necessary to produce a quick list of this sort to see that there is no shortage of accountability mechanisms of assorted kinds. A traditional accountability, through Parliament, seems to have been replaced by a dense thicket of largely extra-parliamentary devices to monitor the activities of government. Perhaps this is simply the parliamentary slack being taken up elsewhere. For example it is difficult now to understand the anxiety expressed in some quarters at the time that the decision made in the 1960s to establish an Ombudsman to hear complaints from citizens about maladministration would usurp the role of Members of Parliament in the redress of grievances. Yet a verdict now might be that Parliament has been almost wholly bypassed as the plethora of regulators and inquirers and inspectorates has been established. Parliament has been an onlooker, not a participant, in this process. Does this matter? If the job is being done, does it matter who is doing it?

It does if Parliament is to perform its function of holding power to account. Parliament should not pretend (as it once did) that it can substitute for other forms of accountability; but it should take steps to ensure that it sits at the apex of accountability. Holding power to account should be a continuous process, on a variety of fronts and involving a range of bodies, but this whole process should be pulled together by the formal institutions of representative democracy. Parliament should watch the watchdogs, inspect the inspectors, audit the auditors, and regulate the regulators. It should work with all these bodies to ensure that the system of accountability is effective, and has an orderly and coherent shape.

What Parliament, uniquely, can insist on is public accountability. It does this routinely in relation to ministers and senior officials, in a process that is fundamental to parliamentary democracy, but also increasingly in relation to other centres of power. It can demand answers, in public, from people who would often prefer not to provide answers, from media moguls to bankers. Its inquiries may be less well equipped to discover the truth than other forms of inquiry (as with phone-hacking, where it took a judicial inquiry to expose the interlocking world of newspaper owners and politicians) and often confuses accountability with the daily political knockabout; but it nevertheless stands for an indispensable form of public and political accountability. The permanent challenge for Parliament (and its reputation) is to show that it really can hold power to account.

Chapter 7
The end of British politics?

> Perhaps historians might record this strange, heady fortnight as the
> moment when we finally laid to rest a national myth that had
> dogged us so long, concluding a narrative that began with one
> London Olympiad and ended in another: the age of decline
> 1948–2012.
>
> (Jonathan Freedland, *Guardian*, 11 August 2012)

When, in 2011, two pandas arrived from China to take up
residence at Edinburgh zoo, wry commentators pointed out that
this meant that there were now more pandas in Scotland than
Conservative Members of Parliament. At general elections in the
1950s the Conservatives had routinely taken nearly half the total
vote in Scotland and a large percentage of the parliamentary seats.
Sixty years later the Nationalists were the governing party in the
new Scottish Parliament and preparing to hold a referendum on
independence.

This was just one of the striking changes in the political life of her
kingdom that Queen Elizabeth II, and her people, might have
reflected on as her Diamond Jubilee was celebrated in 2012.
Indeed the monarchy's survival and durability could be seen,
despite some wobbles, as a singular monument to continuity in a
shifting political world. The Queen's first prime minister, Winston
Churchill, had presided over a wartime coalition; but her latest

(and twelfth) prime minister, David Cameron, was the only one to head a peacetime one, the first for eighty years. The failure of the 2010 general election to produce a majority single-party government marked a decisive rupture in the post-war pattern of British party politics.

Yet it was a rupture that had been long presaged, in the fracturing of political allegiance over preceding decades. At the general election of 1951, the year before the Queen's accession, the two-party system of Conservative and Labour accounted for 97 per cent of votes that were cast. Sixty years later, at the general election of 2010, that figure had plummeted to 65 per cent. Only the working of the electoral system had kept up the appearance of two-party politics in governing terms. This same story of political fracture and fragmentation can be told in a different way, in terms of the diminished share of the vote won by parties that did secure governing majorities. In 1951 the Conservatives won the election by 26 seats with 48 per cent of the vote; in 2005 Labour won the election by 64 seats with 35 per cent of the vote. Even when parties won outright, it was on the basis of much reduced popular support. This in turn raised questions about legitimacy and governing authority.

So the arrival of coalition government in 2010, bringing together Conservatives (with 306 seats and 36 per cent of the vote) and Liberal Democrats (57 seats and 23 per cent of the vote), looked less like an aberration and more like the culmination of long-developing trends. If this was so, then it might represent the new political normality. It would also represent a repudiation of some of the old axioms of British political life: that the British do not have coalitions, do not like them, and have an electoral system that prevents them. In fact these axioms were only the conventional wisdom of the post-1945 world, which itself began to look aberrant when set against a longer historical perspective, when coalition was more commonplace. Even if the experience of coalition government eventually nurtured a popular desire to return to the governing simplicity of majoritarian single-party rule, the reality of a more fractured electorate would remain.

What coalition did involve was an altered style of politics. It was more difficult to sustain a traditional adversarialism when parties were required to work together. A more European-style politics of negotiation, deal-making, and coalition-building was called for (in political science terms, less 'majoritarian' and more 'consensual'), which some found refreshing and others irksome. This had already been built, by design, into the devolved assemblies that had been created, but it now found itself (by necessity, not design) taking root at Westminster too. It might bring with it a loss of governing coherence, and was open to the charge that it produced a government that nobody had voted for, but it also offered an antidote to the routinized adversarialism that had for so long dominated British politics.

If there was to be a different kind of politics, then it brought with it significant implications. For example, party manifestos could no longer be regarded as political holy writ, a binding contract with the electorate, but as bargaining positions to take into coalition negotiations. Even the argument about the Westminster electoral system would have to change, notwithstanding the emphatic rejection by referendum in 2011 of the Alternative Vote proposal that had been part of the coalition deal with the Liberal Democrats. It was no longer possible to argue that change to the political system would only come from change to the electoral system, as change had clearly happened. Now the argument for electoral reform had to be that it was because politics had changed that the electoral system had to change to reflect the new reality.

If there was little popular enthusiasm for this argument, it was in part because there was little popular enthusiasm for politics itself. The old ideological antagonisms that had sustained political life for much of the twentieth century had become eroded, party memberships had slumped, and allegiances weakened (except on

14. 'A new politics'? David Cameron and Nick Clegg enter coalition, May 2010

the political fringes). Political leaders tried out new narratives—Tony Blair's 'third way', David Cameron's 'big society'--but found little popular resonance. The politics of austerity that has followed the financial crisis has flattened political optimism. An Ipsos Mori poll at the end of 2011 found a new pessimism in Britain, with 61 per cent of people saying that the country was getting worse as a place to live and only 23 per cent believing that their children would have a higher quality of life than themselves. Pessimism nourishes disengagement (or varieties of extremism). Without the

15. 'Or new tensions?' (Gary Barker, *The Guardian*, 5 January, 2012)

plausible promise of a better tomorrow, the appeal of politics and politicians is inevitably diminished.

Yet the disengagement from politics (or at least from the formal political system) had preceded these recent events, which merely served to intensify it. This is seen most sharply in electoral turnout. In the first election of the Queen's reign in 1955 it was 77 per cent; in 2010 it was 65 per cent (having slumped to under 60 per cent in 2001), despite the prospect of a change of government and the stimulus of the first ever televised debates between the party leaders. Taken together with the decline of party membership and weakening of party allegiance, this seemed to indicate a general political disengagement which has prompted much agonizing and inquiry-holding. The fact that this trend was not confined to Britain did not make it less troubling. The title of a recent book by a British political scientist—*Why We Hate Politics*—caught the mood.

The problem was easier to identify than to explain, though, while remedies were even more elusive. Fewer people (especially younger ones) now saw electoral participation as a civic duty. There was less intense ideological competition between the parties, less attachment to them, and political choice was more muted. There was, perhaps, a feeling born out of experience that the problems remained the same whichever party won an election (and that, unlike the prevailing consumer culture, politics brought only disappointments). There was something else too, though, which marked the distance between the beginning of the Queen's reign and her Diamond Jubilee. This was the extent to which the power of action of a British government had been reduced, both deliberately and by necessity. Power had been contracted out—to regulators, markets, Brussels, judges, and elsewhere—while the balance of global economic and political power had shifted in a way that had made Britain count for less. In a whole variety of ways power seemed to have gone elsewhere. As former prime minister John Major put it in his memoirs: 'Governments can cajole, entice or plead, but they can no longer control.' Perhaps people have concluded that, if governments can do less, they can be attended to less.

Or it may be, as some argue, that the British political culture has been inimical to popular participation, the product of a power structure that has been uniquely centralized and concentrated. On this view the remedy for political malaise is a bracing dose of political reform that will open up new opportunities for participation. So there are demands for more referendums (with membership of the European Union as a perennially favourite topic), primary elections to expand the range of political choice, and for electoral reform to make all votes count. There are proposals for elected mayors in cities, and for elected police commissioners; and, in some circumstances, for the popular recall of disgraced MPs. What all such proposals have in common is a break from the traditional British way of doing politics and a borrowing of models from elsewhere.

What they also have in common is a reaction to the sense that politics is increasingly the preserve of a professional political class, with the leading participants looking and sounding very much like each other, with no real experience outside politics and competing only to be in office. The erosion of the social basis of politics, the connecting rods to the wider society, both explains and compounds this development. Among the political class the privately educated are vastly over-represented; the working class now hardly represented at all. One reaction is therefore to seek ways to wrest politics away from the political class, through various devices of direct democracy; although this kind of populism brings its own abundant difficulties. Another reaction is for the electorate to seek political leaders who at least seem to bring that elusive quality of authenticity to the role.

The fact that there is said to be a political malaise in Britain, prompting calls for assorted reforms, might seem to represent a failure of the sweeping constitutional reforms introduced by the Labour government elected in 1997. These were intended to remedy what was widely seen as the quintessential British political problem, which was the concentration of unchecked and unconstitutionalized executive power (famously described in the language of 'elected dictatorship'). In this these reforms have been remarkably successful. Much more of the constitution has been codified, many areas that were traditionally unregulated have been regulated, and a plethora of monitory bodies has been established. In all sorts of ways and on a range of fronts power has been checked, constrained, and divided up.

A British government now has to share, or yield, power to other governments in the different countries of the union, as well as to the EU. Its policies and actions are increasingly challenged in the courts. It is surrounded by scrutineers, regulators, and watchdogs. A traditional secrecy of official information is replaced by an enforced openness. Even in its semi-reformed state the House of Lords has more confidence in asking governments to think again.

At the same time the House of Commons has shown itself to be more assertive, claiming more powers, and with MPs less willing than was once the case simply to toe the party line. This makes party management—and the life of governments—more difficult. With the arrival of coalition government, power now also has to be divided within itself.

What all this means is that traditional descriptions of British politics have to be revised. A political system that was once distinguished by its governing simplicity has become much more complicated. When the young Queen came to the throne, its operation could have been easily explained to her. One of two parties, who between them were supported by almost the entire electorate, with this support neatly divided on class lines, would win an election and form a government. It would govern through its secure control of the House of Commons, where it would also be held to account. Its conduct would be framed by a set of governing conventions understood and accepted by the participants. The House of Lords would bow to its authority, as would the courts. It controlled the flow of official information. Its governing authority encompassed the whole of Britain (and beyond). Armed with the constitutional doctrine of parliamentary sovereignty, conveying the democratic will of the electorate, a government could govern without let or hindrance. It could then, if the electorate so decided, be booted out and replaced with the alternative government.

Such simplicity has now gone, never to return. The next monarch will require a much more complicated explanation of how Britain is governed. This was not the result of a conscious plan, or a new constitutional settlement (as Anthony King puts it, 'we have, if anything a new constitutional unsettlement'), but the product of a whole series of disparate developments. For example, joining the Common Market (as it then was) was seen—on all sides—as essential for Britain's economic future; introducing devolution as necessary for keeping Scotland within the union; and legislating on human rights as 'bringing rights home' from Strasbourg. Yet none of such developments has been without consequences or controversy. The argument about whether membership of the EU brings pooled or lost sovereignty is more intense than ever. Human rights law has brought judges and Parliament into conflict, prompting calls for the legislation and its operation to be revisited. Meanwhile Tony Blair has regretted introducing freedom of information law ('I quake at the imbecility of it') because it makes governing more difficult. What all this demonstrates is that a traditional political model may have gone; but a durably settled new one has not yet been established.

Nowhere is this clearer than in relation to Britain itself. The Queen's accession coincided with the high-water mark of Britishness, as a unity transcending diversity, recently fortified by the solidarity of war and the enterprise of making a better post-war world. Sixty years on, the political future of Britain itself is in question. Issues about identity, familiar elsewhere but not in Britain, have become politically salient, prompted both by a much more diverse population and by the dynamic of devolution. On one side there is the UKIP demand for British secession from the EU; on the other side the Nationalist demand for Scottish secession from Britain. As prime minister Gordon Brown desperately (and unsuccessfully) tried to promote a positive conversation about 'Britishness' in the face of these tendencies. While the Scots contemplated independence, and the Welsh demanded the sort of devolution the Scots had, the English began to ask where all this left them. It was a messy picture, both in terms of identities and structures. Here, too, simplicity had been replaced by complexity. The character of 'British' politics is changing; and may soon need a different name.

The reality is that Britain is several countries, even if (for the moment) a single state; and with a complex cultural diversity. Much of the ancestral glue of Britishness, not least that associated with empire and war, has dissolved; and it is not clear whether—and how—a new kind of glue can be put together. In the course of 2012, the combined impact of the Jubilee and, more significantly, the London Olympics was to promote much excited commentary about the revival of a confident and capacious Britishness with a contemporary rather than merely nostalgic resonance. As Robert McCrum, reflecting this commentary, expressed it: 'Now the patriotic bounce from the Olympics has had this unexpected outcome: suddenly we're all Britons again' (*Observer*, 19 August 2012). Only time would tell if this was true, or how long it would last, and what its political implications might be.

In terms of the structure of the state, there was speculation about the effect on support for Scottish independence to be tested in the referendum scheduled for 2014. If Britain does stay together, it is likely that there will be further development towards a sort of quasi-federalism. As Gladstone declared in 1879: 'If we can make arrangements under which Ireland, Scotland, Wales, portions of England, can deal with questions of local and special interest to themselves more efficiently than parliament now can, that, I say, will be the attainment of a great national good.' However, 'portions of England' show no sign yet of wanting to join the devolutionary feast. There is much talk of the English Question, but usually in terms of the alleged unfairness of Scottish MPs being able to vote on matters affecting England while English MPs are not able to vote on matters devolved to Scotland. There have been various proposals to deal with this, from an English parliament to procedural changes at Westminster, but none are without their own difficulties. These are the consequences of a lop-sided union with one overwhelmingly dominant partner. Some have therefore concluded that, at least for the moment, the English Question is best left unanswered (or unasked). Meanwhile the English seem quite content for the Scots to go their own way, if that is what they want, while hoping that they will prefer to stay.

It is only necessary to describe these developments in British politics for it to be seen how much has changed and in such a relatively short time. Politics in Britain has regularly in the past been described as being 'in transition', but in this period it undoubtedly has been. It is not just that simplicity has, in so many respects, been replaced by complexity (and this includes the way in which services provided by the state are now organized); but also that the general characterization of the political system has to be revised. If, in the last decade of the twentieth century, the charge against the system was that the executive was too powerful and unchecked—in short, that there was too much government and not enough accountability—by the second decade of the twenty-first century the charge was almost reversed.

Now what was remarked upon was a lack of political coherence and governing capacity. Nor was this merely a function of coalition government (or the inexperience of political leaders), but of a much longer process of political fragmentation and the development of new institutional and other constraints on what governments can do. Governing had become more difficult; and the government machine did not seem to have its old confidence or authority. Even the charge about spin and control-freakery that had been levelled against the Blair government was turned on its head. Now the charge was that the political class had become the slavish servants of the press barons, notably the Murdoch empire.

This is a reminder of the series of seismic shocks that the political system has been hit by in short order, the consequences of which are still working themselves out. The financial crisis of 2008 was not caused by the state, but it did represent a failure to regulate properly and needed massive state intervention to bail out the banks and prevent total economic meltdown. It has been followed by a painful politics of debt reduction and austerity that has choked off economic recovery. Then the scandal of parliamentary expenses in 2009 rocked parliament to its foundations and discredited the whole political class. On top of all that came the revelations about the scale of illegal phone-hacking by sections of the press, with the result that in 2011 a judicial inquiry was established to look at the whole conduct of the press, including its relationship with politicians and the police, which has not presented an edifying picture to public view.

Against this background it is scarcely surprising if the financial class, the political class, and the media class have all suffered a loss of public confidence; and that people are much less trusting of what they say and do. This in turn prompts a further turning away from the public into the private, deepening a trend that was already in evidence. Perhaps this will change if these recent events produce reform and improvement on all the fronts that have been so badly damaged. It may also require a political narrative to emerge that can rise to the level of events. Both left and right (and not just in Britain) seem to have lost their footing in the face of problems that appear bigger than the available solutions. There is no shortage of policy challenges and public discontents, but not yet the kind of convincing political narrative that might provide the basis for the renewal of politics itself.

If British politics is more complicated it is, in great part, because British society is far more complicated than it was when the Queen began her reign sixty years ago. Then the class basis of politics was fundamental; but now the class structure is much more variegated and the link between class and party, though still significant, is less straightforward. In Britain class is never far away, but it is more complicated than it once was. There is also a striking contrast between the drive to reduce inequality in the post-war period, widely shared as a political objective, and the acceleration of inequality in recent decades (reflected in a disconnected underclass and an equally disconnected supra-class), with OECD figures showing this trend to be more marked in Britain than elsewhere in Europe. Why this has happened, what its consequences are, and whether there is either the will or ability to do anything about it, is a matter for political debate.

More generally, the political world of the 1950s—which essentially turned on the battle between socialism and anti-socialism, rooted in the cleavage of class—has been replaced by a middling sort of politics which worries about the country's economic future (which means its ability to secure employment, opportunity, and prosperity for its people) and the cohesion of its society. A range of modern concerns demand political attention and policy response, but many of these issues involve a politics of behaviour, which is inherently more intractable than traditional policy-making, and difficult ethical choices. They also often sit outside the old battle grounds of left and right. Meanwhile a society that has become multicultural (whether as description or prescription) throws up a range of complex and contested issues that were largely absent—except as racism—in the more homogeneous society of sixty years earlier.

The change in social attitudes has been profound, with a direct impact on the conduct of political life. It is a coarser society, less mannered and respectful, with a weaker sense of community; but there is also much less deference and more tolerance of diversity. The role of women has been transformed. There is less trust; and more demand for answers. There is less secrecy and more transparency. All this has changed the terms of trade in political life. Gone is the oleaginous political interview of old, in which the minister was given obsequious thanks just for coming along and being prepared to answer any questions at all. Now politicians are the butt of merciless mockery and scathing interrogation. In the 1950s the BBC was still adhering to a 'fourteen days' rule under which it agreed not to broadcast discussions on any issue which was due to be debated in Parliament during the next fortnight. Now round-the-clock commentary is emitted from every kind of media orifice. In the 1950s it was possible to keep much from public view, including the incapacity of Churchill in his final period of office. Now everything and everyone is fair game.

Yet despite all this change, on so many fronts, the outward appearance of British politics still looks reassuringly familiar. It is rather like the duck appearing calm on the surface of the water while the furious paddling goes on underneath. Notwithstanding the fragmentation of political support, the Conservative and Labour parties still dominate seats in the House of Commons. Ideological division may have become muted, but the party battle is waged much as it was sixty years ago. Despite the transformation that has taken place in the way that state provision is organized, ministerial responsibility to Parliament remains the formal route through which political accountability is exercised. The relationship between ministers and civil servants has survived changes in the nature of government. The House of Lords may have (mostly) swapped inheritance for patronage, but it survives in both name and function. New electoral systems have been developed for new institutions, but for Westminster the first-past-the-post system still endures. Parties may have experienced a severe membership decline, but this diminished party membership still provides the recruitment channel for politicians. In constitutional terms, some powers have been separated out, devolved, formalized, and written down, but much of the constitution remains uncodified and muddles along as it has always done.

Even the arrival of coalition government at Westminster in 2010 was, in its construction, absorbed by a governing tradition that emphasized the imperative that the Queen's government had to be carried on. A hastily assembled coalition agreement provided its underpinning. Even the governing convention of collective responsibility, honed for single-party government, made the transition to coalition government more or less intact. There were increasing strains within the coalition; and plenty of questions about the future. Would the coalition survive as electoral reckoning beckoned and the need for separate political identities became more acute? Would the Liberal Democrats survive (or split into their social liberal and market liberal wings)? Would coalition become the norm or would majoritarian government make a comeback? Could any government get re-elected in the face of prolonged economic austerity and a disgruntled electorate? Would there be alternating one-term governments rather than extended periods of rule by one party (or one coalition)? Yet these future questions sat alongside the fact that, for the moment at least, a traditional way of governing had managed to adapt to new political environment.

This quality of adaptability had long been claimed as a distinctive feature of the British political tradition, explaining its continuity. It had made the historic adaptation to an enlarged franchise in 1832, thereby avoiding a revolutionary break, and had gone on making adaptations ever since. Some of these—notably, membership of the European Union and the incorporation into law of the human rights convention—have involved major alterations in the conduct of government. It had adapted to the rise (and decline) of a class-based ideological politics, and to the changing role of the state. It had adjusted to the exigencies of war, and to the legacy of empire. It had retained a monarchy (despite the forced abdication of a monarch) while becoming a disguised republic. Now it was being required to adjust to the shifting contours of Britain itself. The question was whether the quality of adaptability—rooted in the maturity of its political culture and the flexibility of its governing arrangements—would continue to enable the British political tradition to respond to the new challenges facing it.

This takes us back to where this book started, in its suggestion that 'politics and government' has provided a plausible answer to the question of what Britain might (amongst other things) best be associated with. In 2011 the *New York Times* columnist David Brooks, writing from London, could tell his readers that Britain's political history provided 'a picture of how politics should work' and that 'The British political system is basically functional while the American is not.' In international assessments of good government, Britain is usually ranked about mid-table in the premier league. If this suggests reasonable performance in the combined enterprise of governing effectively and holding power to account, it also identifies the scope for improvement. There is no shortage of critics of the way in which government in Britain works (including Tony Blair, who declared in his memoirs that 'the way we run Westminster or Whitehall today is just not effective in a twenty-first century world'); and no shortage of voices—like that of Democratic Audit and others—documenting the system's democratic deficiencies and identifying the need for further reform.

However, this may be a too sanguine and sober note on which to end this short account of British politics. The real challenge today for the British political tradition comes not so much from the policy and institutional issues with which it is confronted, but from the rise of an anti-politics that repudiates the enterprise of politics itself. In the 2012 report of the Hansard Society's annual *Audit of Political Engagement*, the number of people saying they were 'very' or 'fairly' interested in politics had slumped by 16 percentage points to stand at only 42 per cent, a decline of nine percentage points and the lowest figure ever recorded in this annual survey. The report's conclusion is that indifference to politics is mutating into something more disturbing and 'suggesting a public that is turning away from national politics'.

It is not necessary to believe that there was once a political golden age (a poll taken at the end of the Second World War also showed a widespread distrust of politicians); but it is necessary to recognize that something significant is happening now. The vitality of a political tradition depends upon enough people feeling that politics matters and that, despite all its frustrations and dissatisfactions, it provides the means whereby a democracy can tackle its problems, provide realistic hope for the future, and hold power to account. Without this, politics becomes the preserve of a political class, while a culture of anti-politics offers a standing invitation to those who trade in dangerous simplicities and repudiate the messy complexities inherent in democratic politics. Perhaps the continuity symbolized by a Diamond Jubilee of a monarch provides a good moment to take stock of the health of a political tradition that has been long regarded as embodying these elementary truths.

Further reading

In compiling this very short reading list, I have chosen fifty books which enable the general reader, or enquiring student, to explore further some of the themes and issues in British politics discussed here. It includes some books mentioned in the text, but others which are not, with a preference for readability (which some political science, alas, is not). It combines the classic with the contemporary. Some books are included simply because I like them. It omits general textbooks on British politics, of which there are many and some of which are excellent (although most now seem to have an aversion to anything resembling joined-up argument in favour of distracting devices designed to make them 'student-friendly', which as a student I would have found extremely irritating). It also includes some books by those who have engaged in British politics, as well as those who have written about it, as this adds some real-world flavour to what is, after all, an activity and not just a study.

Walter Bagehot, *The English Constitution* (1867, many editions, including M. Taylor ed., Oxford: OUP, 2009).

Tim Bale, *The Conservative Party from Thatcher to Cameron* (Cambridge: Polity, 2010).

Rodney Barker, *Political Ideas in Modern Britain: In and After the Twentieth Century* (London: Routledge, 1997).

Samuel Beer, *Modern British Politics* (London: Faber, 1965).

Martin Bell, *A Very British Revolution: The Expenses Scandal and How to Save our Democracy* (London: Icon, 2009).

Tom Bingham, *The Rule of Law* (London: Allen Lane, 2010).

A. H. Birch, *Representative and Responsible Government* (London: George Allen and Unwin, 1964).

Tony Blair, *A Journey* (London: Hutchinson, 2010).

Vernon Bogdanor, *The New British Constitution* (Oxford: Hart, 2009).

Gyles Brandreth, *Breaking the Code: Westminster Diaries* (London: Weidenfeld and Nicolson, 1999).

Rodney Brazier, *Constitutional Practice: The Foundations of British Government* (3rd edn., Oxford: OUP, 1999).

David Butler and Gareth Butler, *Political Facts* (10th edn., Basingstoke: Palgrave Macmillan, 2010).

Alastair Campbell, *Diaries* (4 vols., London: Hutchinson, 2010–12).

Philip Cowley, *The Rebels: How Blair Mislaid his Majority* (London: Politico's, 2005).

Alistair Darling, *Back from the Brink* (London: Atlantic Books, 2011).

Democratic Audit, *2012 Audit* (available on-line, <http://democracy-uk-2012.democraticaudit.com>).

David Denver et al, *Elections and Voters in Britain* (3rd edn., Basingstoke: Palgrave Macmillan, 2012).

Roger Eatwell and Matthew Goodwin (eds.), *The New Extremism in 21st Century Britain* (London: Routledge, 2010).

Matthew Flinders et al., *The Oxford Handbook of British Politics* (Oxford: OUP, 2009).

Paul Flynn, *How to be an MP* (London: Biteback, 2012).

Andrew Gamble, *Between Europe and America: The Future of British Politics* (Basingstoke: Palgrave Macmillan, 2003).

Colin Hay, *Why We Hate Politics* (Cambridge: Polity, 2007).

Robert Hazell (ed.), *Constitutional Futures Revisited: Britain's Constitution to 2020* (Basingstoke: Palgrave Macmillan, 2008).

Richard Heffernan et al. (eds.), *Developments in British Politics 9* (Basingstoke: Palgrave Macmillan, 2011; and previous volumes in this series).

Peter Hennessy, *The Prime Ministers: The Office and its Holders since 1945* (London: Penguin, 2001).

Ian Holliday et al., *Fundamentals in British Politics* (Basingstoke: Macmillan, 1999).

Jeffrey Jowell and Dawn Oliver (eds.), *The Changing Constitution* (6th edn., Oxford: OUP, 2007; and previous editions).

David Judge, *Representation: Theory and Practice in Britain* (London: Routledge, 1999).

Dennis Kavanagh and Philip Cowley, *The British General Election of 2010* (Basingstoke: Palgrave Macmillan, 2010).

Anthony King, *The British Constitution* (Oxford: OUP, 2007).

Jack Lively and Adam Lively (eds.), *Democracy in Britain: A Reader* (Oxford: Blackwell, 1994).

John Lloyd, *What the Media are Doing to our Politics* (London: Constable, 2004).

Iain McLean, *What's Wrong with the British Constitution?* (Oxford: OUP, 2010).

John Major, *The Autobiography* (London: HarperCollins, 1999).

David Marquand, *Britain since 1918: The Strange Career of British Democracy* (London: Weidenfeld and Nicolson, 2008).

Chris Mullin, *Diaries* (3 vols., Profile, 2009–11).

Philip Norton, *Parliament in British Politics* (Basingstoke: Palgrave Macmillan, 2005).

Jonathan Powell, *The New Machiavelli* (London: Bodley Head, 2010).

Lance Price, *Where Power Lies: Prime Ministers v. the Media* (New York: Simon and Schuster, 2010).

Frank Prochaska, *The Republic of Britain* (London: Allen Lane, 2000).

Andrew Rawnsley, *The End of the Party: The Rise and Fall of New Labour* (London: Viking, 2010).

R. A. W. Rhodes, *Understanding Governance* (Buckingham: Open University Press, 1997).

Peter Riddell, *Parliament under Blair* (London: Politico's, 2000).

Meg Russell, *The House of Lords: Bicameralism in Modern Britain* (Oxford: OUP, forthcoming).

Anthony Sampson, *Who Runs This Place? The Anatomy of Britain in the 21st Century* (London: John Murray, 2004).

Gerry Stoker, *Why Politics Matters: Making Democracy Work* (Basingstoke: Palgrave Macmillan, 2006).

Stephen Wall, *A Stranger in Europe: Britain and the EU from Thatcher to Blair* (Oxford: OUP, 2008).

Paul Webb, *The Modern British Party System* (London: Sage, 2000).

Paul Whiteley, *Political Participation in Britain* (Basingstoke: Palgrave Macmillan, 2011).

Tony Wright, *Doing Politics* (London: Biteback, 2012).

NB: The Parliament and Constitution Centre at the House of Commons Library produces invaluable Research Papers and Standard Notes on many aspects of British politics which are available on line (<www.parliament.uk>).

Index

A

accountability 16
  and authority 55
  checks and balances 20, 23, 66–7
  informal process of 95
  ministers 57, 60, 87, 95
  Parliamentary 87, 95
  reformed second chamber 99
Acheson, Dean 11
Act of Settlement (1701) 19, 56
adaptation 8
adversarialism 25, 76, 106
Alternative Vote proposal 57, 106
Amery, Leo 41
Anglo-Irish Treaty (1921) 26
Armstrong, Sir William 58
Ashdown, Paddy 73
Asquith, Herbert Henry 6
Attlee, Clement 9, 35–7, 42–4,
  46, 84

B

Bagehot, Walter 19, 21, 73
Balfour, Arthur James 10
Bank of England 30, 52, 61,
  68, 113
BBC 10, 92, 116
Beer, Samuel 40, 96

'big society' 50, 107
Bill of Rights (1689) 18
Bingham, Tom 32
Blackstone, Sir William 20
Blair, Tony 49–50, 63, 88, 90,
  107, 119
  Cabinet meetings 61–2
  on constitutional reform 28–9, 68
  on European integration 48
  and Gordon Brown 58, 59,
    61–2, 64
  and Iraq 96
  selection as parliamentary
    candidate 71
  and strong government 52, 67
  'the King in Parliament' 53
Blairism 46–7
Bogdanor, Vernon 33
Bolingbroke, Henry St John 1st
  Viscount 20
Brandreth, Gyles 90
Bright, John 2
Britain 6–7
British National Party (BNP) 75
British Empire 10
Brown, Gordon 19, 46, 58, 61, 62,
  64, 112
Bryson, Bill 5–6
Burke, Edmund 39, 72, 83
Butler, Sir Robin 61–2

C

Cabinet 54, 58–9, 92
  accountability 60, 89, 95
  collective responsibility 57
  divisions within 58
  questions to 86–7
Cabinet Manual, The 19
Cameron, David 9, 12, 26, 49, 50,
    62, 63, 65, 105, 107
candidate selection 72, 80
capitalism 40, 50–1
Carlisle, Kenneth 87
catch-all parties 84
centralization 13, 45, 53, 67, 68
Channon, 'Chips' Sir Henry 42, 93
Churchill, Sir Winston 2, 3, 9, 42,
    73, 104
civil service 60–64
class division 10, 40, 47
Clegg, Nick 33, 107
coal mines 17
coalition politics 37, 72, 73, 78,
    79, 105
collective cabinet responsibility
    57, 58
collectivism 38–9, 40, 42
Committee on Standards in Public
    Life 68, 82
'common good' 38, 40
Common Market 26, 57, 111
commonality 11–12
conservatism 39, 40, 43, 45
Conservative/Liberal Democrat
    Coalition 32, 50, 52, 57, 62–3,
    65, 82, 92, 95, 96, 99, 105
Conservative Party 73, 74, 75–6
  internal divisions 58
  and local government 66
  party management 81–3
  pit closures policy 17
  race politics 47
  Thatcher revolution 28, 43–45
constituencies 88, 90
constitution 10, 18

and EU membership 27
and parliamentary
    sovereignty 23
traditional balanced 21
Constitution Unit 63
constitutional legislation 19, 25–6
constitutional reform 28–31, 68
Corn Laws 57
crises 10

D

Daily Telegraph 2
Darling, Alistair 52
Davies, Norman 5
debate 90, 92
delegates 83
delivery mechanisms 64
democratic politics 13, 14,
    79, 120
devolution 7, 12, 28, 30, 66, 78
Dicey, A. V. 19, 23, 24, 53
Dickens, Charles 19
Disraeli, Benjamin 9, 39
division lobbies

E

economic management 43
Electoral Commission 30, 38,
    68, 82
electoral systems 30, 54
  first-past-the-post 25, 76
  proportional representation 25
Elizabeth II, Queen 12, 104, 108,
    111, 112, 115
England 5–7
equality 40, 43
European Convention on Human
    Rights 30
European Union 7
  and British constitution 26–7
  and identity politics 48–9, 118
  institutions of the 67, 110
  regionalization 11

and Thatcherism 43
policy control 69
Euroscepticism 8
Eurozone 27, 48
exceptionalism 16
executive 66
  questions to 90
  sovereignty 57 *see also* Cabinet;
    prime minister
extremism 12

F

federalism 68
female suffrage 26
financial crisis 50, 52, 69,
  107, 114
finances for political parties *see*
    party politics, funding
first-past-the-post electoral
    system 26, 76
flexibility 8, 23, 29, 55
Foot, Michael 35
Freedom of Information Act
    (2000) 68
French Revolution 38
Friedman, Milton 43

G

general elections 70, 74, 104
Giddens, Anthony 46
Gladstone, William Ewart 9, 113
Glorious Revolution (1688) 20
Good Friday Agreement (1998) 5
governance 64–5
government:
  departmental basis of 58–62
  and European Union 67–8
  internal division in 58
  scrutiny of legislation 93
  select committees 94
  simplicity of 12–3, 15, 55
  strong 13, 52–7, 64–5, 67, 74, 77
  weaknesses in 67

Graham, Sir James 72
Great Reform Act (1832) 15
Greenleaf, W. H. 38
Green Party 75–6
Guardian 6, 16, 36–7, 78–9

H

Hailsham, Lord 28
Hansard 86, 87
Hayek, Friedrich von 43
Heath, Edward 28
Hennessy, Peter 8, 59, 64
hereditary peers *see* House of Lords
Heseltine, Michael 17
Hoggart, Simon 36
Home Rule 26
House of Commons 11, 92
  accountability 99–100
  constitutional legislation 25
  continuity of 9
  daily business 92
  MP's voting in 93–4
  party politics and 70
  point of order 18
  pre-eminence of 54–5
  Reform Committee 97
  resolution on ministerial
    responsibility 59–60
  scrutiny of legislation 93
  and traditional balanced
    constitutionalism 21
House of Lords 8, 30, 80, 93, 99,
  110, 111, 117
  end of hereditary peers 30
  Parliament Act (1911) 23, 26
  reform of 33, 54, 95, 99
  scrutiny of legislation 93
Human Rights Act (1998) 30, 68
Humphreys, John 101

I

identity politics 48
ideology 37–41, 45, 46, 48

Index

immigration 48
industrial action 43
inflation 43
interest rates 30, 61, 68
Iraq 46, 60, 62, 96
Ireland 6, 26, 113
Irish Question 4
Israel 18

J

Jenkins Commission 73
Joseph, Sir Keith 43
judiciary 14
junior ministers 92

K

Keir, D. L. 6
King, Anthony 4, 31, 54, 111

L

Labour Party 11, 74
   accountability 102
   Attlee revolution 42
   constitutional reforms 29
   emergence of 73
   internal divisions 58
   nadir 75
   party management 81-3
   pit closures 17
   race politics 47-8, 75
   SDP split 75
   and Tony Blair 45, 47,
      48, 61
   women MPs 80
laissez-faire 40
Laski, Harold 41
law 14
   constitutional 25
   European 26
Lawson, Nigel 35, 58
left/right ideologies 37-43
legislation 90

   scrutiny of 93
legislature 56, 88
Liberal Democrats 33, 73,
      76, 78, 82-3, 99,
      105-6, 117
Liberal Party 73-5, 80
liberalism 38-41
local government 45, 66
localism 65-6
London 11
London Assembly 30

M

McCrum, Robert 113
Macmillan, Harold 40
Major, John 58, 62, 68,
      95, 109
mandate doctrine 78-9
manifestos 78-9
Marxism 39
Mathiot, André 2
media 37
   and accountability 100
Melbourne, Lord 57
Members of Parliament 90, 91
   women 80
micro-management 65
Miliband, Ed 9, 50
Ministerial Code 60
ministerial responsibility 60, 66
ministers see Cabinet; junior
      ministers
minority governments 73
Mitchell, Austin 88
mixed government 20
modern party system 72, 79
   see also party politics
monarchy 8, 21
   continuity of 104
   Crown-in-Parliament
      arrangement 13, 55
monetarism 43
Monetary Policy Committee 30,
      61, 68

British Politics

Montesquieu, Charles-Louis de
    Secondat 20
multiculturalism 12
multiparty systems 78

N

nation state 8
National Audit Office 95
national debate 90
National Health Service 11, 36
nationalization 42
New Labour 45, 47, 50, 80
New Right 43, 45
New Zealand 18
Northern Ireland 4, 6, 11, 29, 30,
    66, 69, 77

O

Office for Budget Responsibility 68
Ombudsmen 102
Orwell, George 5, 10

P

Parliament:
    accountability 88, 93, 94, 98,
        99, 100, 102
    executive control of 92
    Members of 90, 91
        women 80
    recall of 109
    State Opening of 9 see also
        House of Commons;
        House of Lords;
        monarchy
Parliament Act (1911) 23, 24, 26
parliamentary expenses
    scandal 70, 96-8, 114
parliamentary majority 13, 15,
    23, 24, 55, 72, 74, 76-7
partisan dealignment 76
party conferences 81
party line 91

party-list elections 81
party politics 24, 25, 70, 74, 77,
    83, 105
    changes to traditional pattern
        of 77, 105
    election manifestos 78
    and the electorate 74
    funding for 19, 30, 68,
        71, 82
    internal divisions 58, 81
    legislation on 71
    media and 37
    membership decline 83, 106
    party management 81-2
    political recruitment process 81
    19th century 72
party whips 91-3
Paxman, Jeremy 101
pluralism 18, 78
political donations 82
political stability 2-3
PPSs (parliamentary private
    secretaries) 92
prerogative powers 53
presentational politics 36-7
pressure groups 93
prime minister 56
    and American presidency 16, 62
    and prerogative powers 53
    weekly question time 90 see also
        Cabinet
private sector watchdogs 101
proportional representation 54
Public Accounts Committee 95
public services 43

R

race politics 47-8, 75
Rawnsley, Andrew 61
referendum 26, 29, 30, 32, 33, 68,
    85, 104, 106, 113, 114
    Common Market (1975) 26-7,
        49, 57, 98, 109
Reform Act (1867) 73

Reform Committee 97
regionalization 11
religious conflict 8
Representation of the People
    Act (1918) 26
resignation 60
Respect Party 75–6
revolution 4, 8, 10
Riddell, Peter 63
Rose, Richard 2
Russell, Lord John 15

S

Scotland 6, 28, 30, 69, 77, 111
Scottish Nationalists 32, 104
Scottish referendum 32, 104, 114
SDP (Social Democratic Party) 75
Second World War 8, 119
sectarian violence 4
Sedgefield 71
Seitz, Raymond 12
select committees 90, 94
separation of powers 15, 20,
    21, 72
single currency 48
Snow, C. P. 14
social class 9–10
social justice 11, 38, 40, 43, 45
socialism 39, 40, 45
soundbites 37
sovereignty:
    executive 55, 56, 57
    and issue of Europe 48
    parliamentary 23, 24, 27,
        79, 88
    of the people 24
Soviet Union 41
Speaker of the House of
    Commons 17–18
speeches 92
spin doctors 36
State Opening of Parliament 9
statecraft 39

strategic capacity 64
Supreme Court 80
Swift, Jonathan 72

T

target-setting 64
Tawney, R. H. 14
Taylor, A. J. P. 10
terrorism 12
Thatcher, Margaret 28, 43–7, 59,
    62, 66
'third way' politics 45, 107
Thorburn, Steve 27
three-party systems 74
Tocqueville, Alexis de 3, 18
top-down politics 40, 41, 53, 81
Toryism 40, 41 see also
    Conservative Party
trade unions 39, 43, 45, 47
Treasury 30, 58, 59, 64
Treaty of Union (1707) 6
trial by jury 79
two-party system 73, 74, 76, 77

U

UK Independence Party
    (UKIP) 49, 75–6, 112
Ulster 7
unemployment 43
United Kingdom 5–7
United States 43, 51
universal suffrage 26, 73

V

Victoria, Queen 56
vote share 75, 76

W

Wales 6, 7, 28, 30, 66, 69,
    75, 77, 113

Wass, Sir Douglas 61
Whitehall 42, 58, 65, 119
welfare state 42
Wilson, Harold 57
Wilson, Sir Richard 64
'winter of discontent' (1978–9) 43
women candidates 80

women MPs 80
working class Conservative
    voters 74

Y

Young, Hugo 16

Index

JOIN OUR COMMUNITY

www.oup.com/vsi

- Join us online at the official Very Short Introductions **Facebook** page.
- Access the thoughts and musings of our authors with our online **blog**.
- Sign up for our monthly **e-newsletter** to receive information on all new titles publishing that month.
- Browse the full range of Very Short Introductions online.
- Read **extracts** from the Introductions for free.
- Visit our library of **Reading Guides**. These guides, written by our expert authors will help you to question again, why you think what you think.
- If you are a teacher or lecturer you can order inspection copies quickly and simply via our website.

Visit the Very Short Introductions website to access all this and more for free.

www.oup.com/vsi

Expand your collection of
VERY SHORT INTRODUCTIONS

1. Classics
2. Music
3. Buddhism
4. Literary Theory
5. Hinduism
6. Psychology
7. Islam
8. Politics
9. Theology
10. Archaeology
11. Judaism
12. Sociology
13. The Koran
14. The Bible
15. Social and Cultural Anthropology
16. History
17. Roman Britain
18. The Anglo-Saxon Age
19. Medieval Britain
20. The Tudors
21. Stuart Britain
22. Eighteenth-Century Britain
23. Nineteenth-Century Britain
24. Twentieth-Century Britain
25. Heidegger
26. Ancient Philosophy
27. Socrates
28. Marx
29. Logic
30. Descartes
31. Machiavelli
32. Aristotle
33. Hume
34. Nietzsche
35. Darwin
36. The European Union
37. Gandhi
38. Augustine
39. Intelligence
40. Jung
41. Buddha
42. Paul
43. Continental Philosophy
44. Galileo
45. Freud
46. Wittgenstein
47. Indian Philosophy
48. Rousseau
49. Hegel
50. Kant
51. Cosmology
52. Drugs
53. Russian Literature
54. The French Revolution
55. Philosophy
56. Barthes
57. Animal Rights
58. Kierkegaard
59. Russell
60. Shakespeare
61. Clausewitz
62. Schopenhauer
63. The Russian Revolution

64. Hobbes
65. World Music
66. Mathematics
67. Philosophy of Science
68. Cryptography
69. Quantum Theory
70. Spinoza
71. Choice Theory
72. Architecture
73. Poststructuralism
74. Postmodernism
75. Democracy
76. Empire
77. Fascism
78. Terrorism
79. Plato
80. Ethics
81. Emotion
82. Northern Ireland
83. Art Theory
84. Locke
85. Modern Ireland
86. Globalization
87. The Cold War
88. The History of Astronomy
89. Schizophrenia
90. The Earth
91. Engels
92. British Politics
93. Linguistics
94. The Celts
95. Ideology
96. Prehistory
97. Political Philosophy
98. Postcolonialism
99. Atheism
100. Evolution
101. Molecules
102. Art History
103. Presocratic Philosophy
104. The Elements
105. Dada and Surrealism
106. Egyptian Myth
107. Christian Art
108. Capitalism
109. Particle Physics
110. Free Will
111. Myth
112. Ancient Egypt
113. Hieroglyphs
114. Medical Ethics
115. Kafka
116. Anarchism
117. Ancient Warfare
118. Global Warming
119. Christianity
120. Modern Art
121. Consciousness
122. Foucault
123. The Spanish Civil War
124. The Marquis de Sade
125. Habermas
126. Socialism
127. Dreaming
128. Dinosaurs
129. Renaissance Art
130. Buddhist Ethics
131. Tragedy
132. Sikhism
133. The History of Time
134. Nationalism
135. The World Trade Organization

136. Design
137. The Vikings
138. Fossils
139. Journalism
140. The Crusades
141. Feminism
142. Human Evolution
143. The Dead Sea Scrolls
144. The Brain
145. Global Catastrophes
146. Contemporary Art
147. Philosophy of Law
148. The Renaissance
149. Anglicanism
150. The Roman Empire
151. Photography
152. Psychiatry
153. Existentialism
154. The First World War
155. Fundamentalism
156. Economics
157. International Migration
158. Newton
159. Chaos
160. African History
161. Racism
162. Kabbalah
163. Human Rights
164. International Relations
165. The American Presidency
166. The Great Depression and The New Deal
167. Classical Mythology
168. The New Testament as Literature
169. American Political Parties and Elections
170. Bestsellers
171. Geopolitics
172. Antisemitism
173. Game Theory
174. HIV/AIDS
175. Documentary Film
176. Modern China
177. The Quakers
178. German Literature
179. Nuclear Weapons
180. Law
181. The Old Testament
182. Galaxies
183. Mormonism
184. Religion in America
185. Geography
186. The Meaning of Life
187. Sexuality
188. Nelson Mandela
189. Science and Religion
190. Relativity
191. The History of Medicine
192. Citizenship
193. The History of Life
194. Memory
195. Autism
196. Statistics
197. Scotland
198. Catholicism
199. The United Nations
200. Free Speech
201. The Apocryphal Gospels
202. Modern Japan
203. Lincoln

204. Superconductivity
205. Nothing
206. Biography
207. The Soviet Union
208. Writing and Script
209. Communism
210. Fashion
211. Forensic Science
212. Puritanism
213. The Reformation
214. Thomas Aquinas
215. Deserts
216. The Norman Conquest
217. Biblical Archaeology
218. The Reagan Revolution
219. The Book of Mormon
220. Islamic History
221. Privacy
222. Neoliberalism
223. Progressivism
224. Epidemiology
225. Information
226. The Laws of Thermodynamics
227. Innovation
228. Witchcraft
229. The New Testament
230. French Literature
231. Film Music
232. Druids
233. German Philosophy
234. Advertising
235. Forensic Psychology
236. Modernism
237. Leadership
238. Christian Ethics
239. Tocqueville
240. Landscapes and Geomorphology
241. Spanish Literature
242. Diplomacy
243. North American Indians
244. The U.S. Congress
245. Romanticism
246. Utopianism
247. The Blues
248. Keynes
249. English Literature
250. Agnosticism
251. Aristocracy
252. Martin Luther
253. Michael Faraday
254. Planets
255. Pentecostalism
256. Humanism
257. Folk Music
258. Late Antiquity
259. Genius
260. Numbers
261. Muhammad
262. Beauty
263. Critical Theory
264. Organizations
265. Early Music
266. The Scientific Revolution
267. Cancer
268. Nuclear Power
269. Paganism
270. Risk
271. Science Fiction
272. Herodotus

273. Conscience
274. American Immigration
275. Jesus
276. Viruses
277. Protestantism
278. Derrida
279. Madness
280. Developmental Biology
281. Dictionaries
282. Global Economic History
283. Multiculturalism
284. Environmental Economics
285. The Cell
286. Ancient Greece
287. Angels
288. Children's Literature
289. The Periodic Table
290. Modern France
291. Reality
292. The Computer
293. The Animal Kingdom
294. Colonial Latin American Literature
295. Sleep
296. The Aztecs
297. The Cultural Revolution
298. Modern Latin American Literature
299. Magic
300. Film
301. The Conquistadors
302. Chinese Literature
303. Stem Cells
304. Italian Literature
305. The History of Mathematics
306. The U.S. Supreme Court
307. Plague
308. Russian History
309. Engineering
310. Probability
311. Rivers
312. Plants
313. Anaesthesia
314. The Mongols
315. The Devil
316. Objectivity
317. Magnetism
318. Anxiety
319. Australia
320. Languages
321. Magna Carta
322. Stars
323. The Antarctic
324. Radioactivity
325. Trust
326. Metaphysics
327. The Roman Republic
328. Borders
329. The Gothic
330. Robotics
331. Civil Engineering
332. The Orchestra
333. Governance
334. American History
335. Networks
336. Spirituality
337. Work
338. Martyrdom
339. Colonial America
340. Rastafari

341. Comedy
342. The Avant-Garde
343. Thought
344. The Napoleonic Wars
345. Medical Law
346. Rhetoric
347. Education
348. Mao
349. The British
     Constitution